Write It Out, Don't Fight It Out

How to Use Letters to Heal Your Relationship When Talking Gets Tough

Barrie Davenport

Disclaimer

Your Free Gift

As a way of saying thank you for your purchase, I'm offering a free companion website that is exclusive to readers of *Write It Out, Don't Fight It Out.*

With the companion website, you'll have access to a collection of printable relationship guides, checklists, couple's questions, and more bonuses. Click or copy the link below to get free instant access.

>>Go Here to Access the Write It Out, Don't Fight It Out Companion Website<<
liveboldandbloom.com/write-not-fight

Contents

About Barrie Davenport

Barrie Davenport is a certified personal coach, thought leader, author, and creator of several online courses on relationships, self-confidence, life passion, habit creation, and self-publishing She is the founder of the top-ranked personal development site, Live Bold and Bloom.com. Her work as a coach, blogger, and author is focused on offering people practical strategies for living happier, more successful, and more mindful lives. She utilizes time-tested, evidence-based, action-oriented principles and methods to create real and measurable results for self-improvement.

You can learn more about Barrie on her Amazon author page at barriedavenport.com/author.

Introduction

Sarah was so infuriated; her head was spinning. How could Jason do this again?

She made dinner arrangements with her parents weeks ago, but at the last minute, her husband, Jason, announced he had to work late and wouldn't be joining them.

It's not the first time this has happened. In fact, it seems that every time she makes plans with her parents, Jason finds a way to wiggle out of them. And every time Sarah tries to talk with him about it, they have a huge fight. Nothing gets settled, and it takes days for things to feel semi-normal between them again.

Sarah feels hurt and disrespected by Jason's behavior and protective of her parents, whom she loves very much. During their fights, she makes angry digs at Jason, accusing him of being selfish and hating her parents.

Jason believes Sarah is too dependent on her parents, and even though he does like them, he doesn't want to spend as much time with them as Sarah does. He's afraid to tell Sarah directly, because she gets so upset, so he ends up finding excuses to get out of the arrangements.

When they argue about the issue, Jason quickly gets defensive and frustrated with Sarah's reaction, and then he shuts down out of exhaustion and feeling overwhelmed. He stonewalls Sarah, until she starts crying and walks away.

They both hold unresolved anger and tension about the topic, but talking about it gets them nowhere. They don't know how to say what they feel and express what they need without the discussion turning ugly and angry.

It's gotten to the point that they avoid talking about it altogether. The subject has become the big elephant in the room, creating a wall of hurt between them. It has eroded some of their closeness and mutual trust.

Sarah and Jason's situation (or something similar) isn't uncommon in marriages and long-term, intimate relationships. Most of us don't enter a relationship with the natural skills to communicate with each other in a way that minimizes conflict and fosters intimacy and growth. We aren't born with these aptitudes, and for many of us, good communication skills weren't modeled for us by our parents.

Healthy, mature communication in your relationship requires the regular practice of sharing concerns, needs, and feelings in an atmosphere of respect and empathy. It also requires navigating conflict and life challenges in a way that doesn't jeopardize the closeness of your connection or undermine trust and security within the relationship.

This is the ideal, but most of us fall short of this ideal when it comes to communicating with our partners. We have our fears, insecurities, and hot buttons that compel us to respond defensively, say things we later regret, or neglect to say things that need to be said.

Maybe you and your partner have stopped really communicating altogether. You're like two ships passing in the night, afraid to talk for fear of how the conversation might turn out. The potential for pain and bitterness is too daunting.

Perhaps your conversations have devolved into constant bickering, stonewalling, or passive-aggressive comments, leaving you both feeling drained and misunderstood.

Barrie Davenport

There's no doubt that communication is difficult in the best of circumstances, but add in a hefty dose of resentment, anger, or defensiveness, and conversation becomes a minefield littered with a thousand potential explosions.

Why is it that we begin a relationship able to talk about anything, sharing our most intimate secrets, and discussing the minutia of our lives—only to eventually wind up in separate corners, unable to connect in this most basic way?

One reason could be our natural tendency to dodge conflict at all costs, biting our tongues or actively taking steps to avoid potential discord. Saying nothing feels safer than dealing with the fallout, even if it means compromising ourselves and our needs. Perhaps we are too distracted by the whirlwind of daily life or too fearful of being judged or rejected to talk openly and honestly.

A more likely scenario is that we simply lack the fundamental skills needed to communicate with our partner or spouse in a healthy, mature, and productive way. No one offered us a communication manual for relationships, and even if they had, would we have read it during the passionate throes of infatuation and new love?

As the infatuation stage fades, we tend to slip into unhealthy communication habits—like making assumptions rather than asking questions, or offering sullen silence rather than straight talk. We find ourselves reacting with words and behaviors that are more suited to a surly teenager than a mature adult who wants to have a successful, happy relationship.

The ability to verbally communicate with your partner in ways that promote closeness, affection, empathy, compassion, and respect involves a set of skills and behaviors that all couples should make the time to learn.

Healthy communication creates a protective barrier, allowing you to head off divisive conflicts and misunderstandings before they erupt. It also reinforces your commitment, intimacy, and love. It's no secret that poor communication between couples is both a cause and a symptom of problems that can ultimately lead to the demise of the relationship.

Learning these healthy skills and adopting them as regular habits is more challenging that it appears. First, you *both* need to be motivated to learn the skills. That in itself can be a problem, as often one partner is motivated and the other isn't. Some couples believe they can figure out how to communicate on the fly, assuming their love will make it easy, only to find out too late that they were missing the necessary tools.

Even when you both are motivated to learn healthy communication skills, you will face intense emotional hot buttons and the eventual relationship inertia that can throw you off track. You also have to navigate years of internal baggage you both bring to the relationship that can make an innocent comment from your partner feel like an attack, or an offhand observation seem like a putdown.

Learning these skills can take time—years maybe. And if you've been married or in a relationship for many years already, with a backlog of unhealthy, hurtful communication habits to overcome, then you have some real work ahead of you.

So where does that leave a couple with communication problems in the here and now? Aside from spending time every week in a therapist's office, how can you and your partner communicate about your needs, hurts, and concerns without it devolving into acrimony?

If you are someone who has a hard time talking about your emotions or feels deeply uncomfortable with conflict or confrontation, is it healthy to keep your thoughts and feelings stuffed inside? Is there a way to work through challenges and express needs with your partner without wounding each other or diminishing yourself?

Yes, there is a way, and it's one that is free, easy, and potentially life-changing for your relationship: writing letters.

I have found in my own intimate relationships and through my work with coaching clients that putting your thoughts and feelings into writing is a highly effective way to communicate and deal with conflict when verbal communication isn't working.

Letter writing also can help you *initiate* verbal communication on a sensitive or difficult topic without the rancor or defensiveness that can be stirred up in a face-to-face conversation. When you are able to put your thoughts and feelings into writing in a calm, kind, and thoughtful way, you can sidestep much of the pain and divisiveness that difficult conversations foster.

Does this mean you should only communicate in writing with your partner? Of course not. One-on-one verbal communication is the ideal way to interact with your partner in most situations—if you can do it in a way that doesn't harm your love and intimacy.

7

But writing can serve as a great enhancement, substitute, or replacement for a challenging discussion when the going gets rough, or when you just find talking too uncomfortable. Let's review why letter writing is a valuable communication tool in your relationship and when you should use it.

Why Letter Writing Works and When to Use It

You may be surprised to discover that the simple act of writing letters to your partner can be a transformational process in healing your relationship and helping you become more self-aware and compassionate. Even if you are the only partner to ever write a word, the power of writing can't be understated.

Let's return for a moment to our scene with Sarah and Jason, who are now in the midst of yet another argument about Sarah's parents and Jason's reluctance to spend time with them.

In less than a few minutes, the conversation has escalated, and both Sarah and Jason are on the defensive and priming their arguments. Neither can hear the other's point of view, or understand the deeper emotions behind their entrenched positions.

But let's imagine that Jason takes a deep breath and stops the argument. He needs a break to calm down and gather his thoughts. Alone in his office, he pulls out a piece of paper and begins to write how he's feeling about the situation and why he feels this way.

He doesn't see Sarah's tense face or hear her angry words. He's alone and can process his thoughts and feelings without the emotional intensity that both of them bring to the table.

The anxiety he feels during his conflicts with Sarah is mitigated by the free expression of his emotions on paper. In his letter, he says . . .

> *Dear Sarah,*
>
> *I love you with all my heart, and I love your parents too. I never want to hurt you, and I'm sorry this topic has become so difficult for both of us. I was wrong to cancel our plans at the last minute, and I'm sorry.*
>
> *I know how strongly you feel about spending time with your family and how important that is to you. That's why it's been hard for me to talk about it and be forthright with you.*
>
> *I need you to understand that sharing my life with you and having our time together is so*

important to me. I do want to spend time with your family on occasion. I want to spend more time with just us and with our circle of friends.

This isn't because I don't want to be with your parents. I enjoy time with them very much. I just don't want to spend as much time with them as you do.

Also, I want you to know how much it hurts when you call me selfish and unloving. It reminds me of the way my dad would cut me off and put me down when I was a kid. I need you to respect my needs without criticizing me, even if you disagree.

Let's find a solution to this that works for both of us. I'd prefer we see your mom and dad once a month as a couple (except on holidays and special occasions when we see them more) and that you ask me before you make the arrangements, to make sure the dates work for me.

Do you understand my feelings? What are your thoughts about this? Please write back and let me know.

Love,
Jason

In his letter, Jason is able to be loving, apologetic, and sincere in a way he can't muster up when he feels hurt and angry during conflict. He is able to state his needs directly without worrying Sarah will diminish him. He has time to think through what he wants to say and to choose his words carefully and mindfully.

He doesn't blame Sarah, but rather talks about how her behaviors make him feel and the past pain it triggers for him. He can initiate negotiation and suggest compromise without stonewalling or putting a stake in the ground about his demands.

For both Jason and Sarah, this letter can deflate the bitterness and tension that was swelling in their discussion. Away from Sarah, Jason can measure his words and avoid knee-jerk reactions.

Reading the letter away from Jason, Sarah can empathize with Jason's feelings and soften her heart based on his vulnerability. She becomes more willing to find a workable solution, especially knowing that Jason's goal is to spend more time with her, not because he hates her parents.

In their separate experiences with the letter, both Jason and Sarah feel relieved and less anxious, although this may be truer for Jason. In fact, research* supports that writing about emotions is a healing process that can relieve stress and trauma, and also strengthen the immune system.

Writing for healing has been studied at length related to journal writing, but the same positive benefits apply when writing a letter to your partner. Writing to your partner allows you to share your feelings, be clear and direct to get your point across, and potentially resolve the conflict.

In reading the letter, your partner also is protected from the heated emotions of face-to-face conflict and can better process your point of view without setting up a counterargument. It leaves room for understanding, compromise, and negotiation.

At the very least, a letter can open the lines of verbal communication with the buffer of an initial written expression, which can soften emotions before you enter a dialogue. It can open the door to a calmer, safer discussion.

The critical thing to remember is that these letters must be written without the judgmental and loaded words that automatically put your partner on the defensive.

---

* An asterisk indicates that a full citation is found in the References section in the back of this book.

Hot-button words and phrases will make them unable to hear the real message you are trying to express. Your partner is bound to counter with an attack, responding with his or her own arsenal of loaded words. For the best chance of a letter triggering a resolution, it's essential to write it correctly, which I will discuss more in the following chapters.

The purpose of letter writing in this context is to make things better—not to find another vehicle for lashing out or continuing an argument. Subtle digs, passive-aggressive comments, demands, criticisms, and anything you know will wound your partner should be left out of the letter.

Your goals should be healing, connection, empathy, compassion, vulnerability, intimacy, compromise, forgiveness, apology, kindness, understanding, respect, and always love. You can still express your needs, ask for a change in behavior, or communicate your boundaries in a productive and kind way.

So when should you use letter writing rather than verbal communication? The general rule of thumb is whenever conversation gets so testy, hurtful, or uncomfortable that you can't discuss the topic openly, maturely, and kindly.

Here are some situations in which letter writing can be highly useful.

- When one or both of you begins to get angry or defensive during a conflict.

- When one or both of you shuts down during a conflict.

- When one of you refuses to discuss a topic.

- When you need to reveal something painful, shameful, or dishonest, and it's too hard to say the words.

- When you need to offer an apology about a sensitive topic.

- When you get so flustered, anxious, or emotional that you can't talk or express yourself well.

- When you want to express a desire or a need about an uncomfortable topic, such as sex or a partner's weight gain, for example.

- When you need to explain yourself or the situation, and it involves a lot of detail or complex information.

- When you need more time to process your thoughts and feelings about the topic.

- When you need to express your opinion or belief about the topic and don't want to be interrupted or distracted.

- If you are someone who finds it difficult to express emotions or formulate thoughts verbally.

- If you are someone who has issues with anger management and doesn't want to lose it during a conversation.

- When you consistently don't feel heard by your partner during conflict or other important conversations.

- When you want to keep a record of what's been expressed and communicated.

- When you fear your partner will react badly, and you want to give him or her time to process before responding.

- When you are in a long-distance relationship or some other situation where verbal communication is difficult.

Write It Out, Don't Fight It Out

You may find many situations for which writing a letter to your spouse or partner becomes your go-to method for communicating. If both of you find this a positive, healing experience, all the better.

According to relationship expert, and bestselling author, Dr. John Gottman, both partners in a relationship are emotionally available to each other only 9 percent of the time. This means that 91 percent of a couple's time together is ripe for miscommunication. When you are writing a letter, or reading one from your partner, you will be more attentive and focused on the message and content.

Even so, please don't neglect verbal communication and building your verbal communication skills, especially when you want to express loving, appreciative words or simply reconnect at the end of the day. Nothing can replace a close, face-to-face conversation for building intimacy.

I offer Support Resources at the end of the book to help you with your verbal communication skills. But for our purposes here, letter writing is a great alternative for times of conflict and discussing difficult topics that make conversation too challenging.

The purpose of this book is to show you how to use letters for difficult or sensitive issues, but you can also use letter writing to express your love, appreciation, and support for your partner. Surprising your partner with a love letter in which you share how much he or she means to you, or detailing what you love and admire about him or her, will enhance your intimacy and bond. A love letter is a special gift you give to your partner that he or she can cherish for years.

According to research* conducted by Dr. Gottman, the ratio of positive interactions to negative interactions with your partner has to be greater than five to one for your relationship to be happy and healthy. In other words, you need five positive, loving encounters to mitigate every negative one.

If you write a letter to your partner about a challenging issue, or if you have a verbal disagreement or do something to hurt your partner, you can use affirming, positive letters as a healing tool. If you need some ideas on how to write a love letter to your partner, you can read this article, "Six Love Letters That Create a Sexier, Happier Relationship"(liveboldandbloom.com/06/relationships/how-to-write-love-letter) on my site, Live Bold and Bloom.

Together Is Better

My recommendation is that you read or at least review this book with your partner. In order for your partner to receive your letters well and respond in kind, he or she needs to understand the purpose of letter writing and how to do it in a constructive way. Mature communication must be a two-way street for the relationship to grow.

In the chapter "How to Use These Letter Writing Templates," I spell out the ground rules for letter writing and how to do it in a way that is healing and positive. The language I use in the letter writing templates is intended to give you words and phrases that are loving, authentic, and kind, even in areas of conflict or hurt.

If you write a letter that you spend time crafting with measured, loving words, and your partner responds with sarcasm, defensiveness, or criticism, then you are stuck in the same difficult place you've been with verbal communication.

Before you write your first letter, make sure your partner understands why this method is valuable, why you want to try it, and how to do it. Show your partner this book, and ask him or her to read it. If your partner refuses, try to explain the core concepts in the book and how to use them. Ask

19

your partner to give it a try with you during times when talking is difficult.

Even if you are the only person writing, or if your partner doesn't respond the way you would like, writing these letters will improve your communication skills and might even eventually influence your partner. In the chapter, "How to Use These Letter Writing Templates," I'll discuss the best ways to respond if your partner doesn't react well to your letters or replies with an unloving letter.

Before we dive into the letter writing scripts, let's talk a bit more about conflict and its place in your relationship.

Why Conflict Is Valuable

One common misconception couples hold is the notion that conflict spells trouble for the relationship. If that were the case, most relationships wouldn't last long. Conflict is inevitable in all relationships.

We bring our own opinions, quirks, and baggage into the relationship, which are bound to trigger discord. Also, life routinely presents us with difficulties and problems that we have to sort out. Even in the happiest, most stable relationships, couples still must face unexpected challenges and differences throughout their lives together that can become sources of conflict.

Conflict itself is not necessarily bad. In fact, relationships that appear conflict free may be unhealthier than those where conflict is more apparent and regular. Stuffing your feelings and sweeping things under the rug only makes the problems bigger. When you avoid conflict, you also bypass a valuable opportunity for strengthening your connection and getting your needs met.

Remember, a conflict isn't always the same as a fight. *A conflict* is an area of disagreement between two partners. *A fight* is a reactionary choice about how you and your partner handle the conflict. Conflict can be deeply destructive, causing resentment, anger, and division. But the good news is that it can also be productive and healing, fostering deeper awareness, intimacy, and respect.

The important factor isn't so much that you have conflict or how often you have it, but rather *how the conflicts are handled and resolved* by both of you. Respect and kindness are the defining variables in keeping conflicts from turning into destructive arguments.

If you change your mindset about conflict, and embrace it as an opportunity for growth and learning, it will be much easier to communicate with each other, whether verbally or in writing, during these challenging occasions.

A 2010 University of Michigan study* revealed that couples in which both partners used constructive conflict strategies, such as letter writing, had lower divorce rates. But the key is that *both partners* must participate.

According to the study,

> *"A particularly toxic pattern is when one spouse deals with conflict constructively, by calmly discussing the situation, listening to their partner's point of view, or trying hard to find out what their partner is feeling, for example -- and the other spouse withdraws."*

This research reinforces the need for both you and your spouse or partner to work together on this letter writing method and support each other in your efforts. You can't resort to the same reactions and habitual responses you use in verbal communication.

One of the main reasons conflict is important is that it signals the need for change in the relationship. Relationships aren't static. You can and should continue to grow and evolve together as a couple and as individuals. If you neglect this call for change, you stunt your growth as partners, and even worse, you set yourselves up for disengagement, resentment, and frustration.

The Deeper Issues behind Conflict

Conflict also helps you and your partner heal or resolve the deeper issues that are frequently behind the issue at hand. Often these deeper issues go back to your childhood and problems you may have had with one or both of your parents.

For example, your frustration with your partner's messiness may have less to do with him or her and more to do with your need for order and control, having felt so out of control as a child. Or your partner's defensiveness when you make suggestions might reveal his underlying feelings that you don't trust or respect him.

As you uncover the deeper reasons behind your conflicts, especially repeat conflicts, you can root out the core issues in your relationship that need healing and attention.

When you unpack these deeper insecurities, fears, or wounds with your partner, and he or she hears them with compassion and respect, you liberate yourself in a way that heals both of you and fosters deeper intimacy. You feel relieved, understood, and accepted, like a weight being lifted from your shoulders. Your partner becomes less reactionary and defensive and can respond more empathetically.

When managed with respect, conflict can build mutual trust, as you are both free to express boundaries and concerns without the fear of judgment, criticism, or blame. You recognize you can have conflict and still come out on the other side unscathed as a couple.

Many of you reading this book may be in the position where verbal conflict invariably turns into a heated argument. Maybe one of you withdraws, or both of you haven't honed the skills of talking it out without anger, defensiveness, or hurt feelings.

You may see the value of conflict, as I've just described it, but in the heated moment, old hurts and insecurities obscure your higher motivations, and you revert to old habits. You're not alone in this—most couples have to work at verbal communication. Because it's so hard and requires restraint, compassion, and selflessness, we tend to do one of two things: we revert to fighting it out, or we avoid outright confrontation by using passive-aggressive behaviors to make our feelings known.

Neither of these options are healthy for your relationship. That's why developing the skill of writing your feelings and needs is so valuable. It gives you an option for healthy conflict that doesn't have to undermine your trust, intimacy, and mutual respect.

Let's move on to cover some of the areas of frustration, misunderstanding, and arguments that are shared by most couples. These are some of the areas where you might find letter writing beneficial.

Common Relationship Conflict Areas

He consistently leaves wet towels on the floor. She makes that weird smacking sound whenever she eats. It's often these little, irritating things that snowball into bigger problems down the road. These little annoyances can eventually grow to signify deeper concerns and needs, making us feel disrespected, unappreciated, ignored, or even unloved.

Every couple has their core conflicts, issues that tend to arise over and over again. The longer they go on, the more difficult it becomes to find a resolution or at least negotiate a compromise that allows the couple to agree to disagree harmoniously.

Dr. Gottman is professor emeritus at the University of Washington, cofounder of the Gottman Institute, and author of more than forty books, including *The Seven Principles for Making Marriage Work.** His studies show that almost 70 percent of relationship conflicts are perpetual (they keep recurring).

Every time you have the argument, it becomes more and more polarizing and emotionally charged. This makes healthy conversation increasingly difficult. You have a hard time discussing the issue with any humor, affection, or empathy for your partner's point of view.

Many of these core conflicts fall into common categories that most couples fight about. As you learn about these common areas of conflict, and recognize the ways you and your partner get embroiled in them, you can focus your letter writing efforts on these linchpin areas first.

As you read through these six areas, make notes about where you and your partner have recurring arguments, or where you might be avoiding conflict that is simmering beneath the surface.

1. Expectations

When we get married or commit to a relationship, we bring our own set of expectations about how the relationship should work and how our partner should behave. You might believe if your husband really loves you, he should know why you are upset without you telling him. Or your wife should be more affectionate because, in your mind, that's what women do.

Many couples have the expectation that love will conquer all and believe the honeymoon phase of the relationship will last forever. They are surprised when eventually their perfect lover doesn't match the idealized version they have clung to.

There are many reasons couples have these expectations. They may have developed as a result of observing their parents' marriages, or because of a fantasy notion about marriage created when each partner was young.

If your parents had a good marriage, then you probably expect yours to be similar. But if your parents divorced or had an unhealthy marriage, you might have developed your own picture of an ideal relationship based on guesswork, media depictions, or your peers.

Whatever the reason you developed them, the expectations of both you and your partner can become a source of conflict when they don't match.

2. Money

Money is often cited as a significant source conflict with couples, regardless of their financial situations. Conflict occurs because our feelings about money reflect our core value systems, and our challenges related to money often reveal our emotional needs for security, trust, and power. Emotional fear can be the fuel for our money fights.

Dr. Gottman suggests these fears include: (1) your fear of not having influence in important issues impacting your life; (2) your fear of not having security in your future; (3) your fear of having no respect shown for your values; or (4) your fear of not realizing your dreams.

Conflicts about money also can relate to one partner earning more than the other, differing financial goals and attitudes, and even personality types.

3. Sex

Most of us don't enter a marriage or committed relationship worried that sex will be a problem. Sexual chemistry is often what draws a couple together in the first place. Eventually, as the honeymoon phase ends, and with children entering the picture, sex can become an area of frustration and conflict.

There is no other part of your lives together that has the potential to cause as much hurt, embarrassment, and feelings of rejection. Couple that with difficulty talking about your sexual frustrations and needs, and you have a perfect storm for conflict.

4. Children

If you have children, you know that as much as you both love them, they can cause disruption and conflict. When a baby enters your lives for the first time, your marriage will change dramatically.

According to Dr. Gottman, 67 percent of women experience a plummet in marital satisfaction after a baby is born. The additional responsibilities of a child, coupled with lack of sleep and hormonal fluctuations, can be fuel for a host of conflicts between a couple.

Another big source of conflict relates to personal freedoms and how each partner spends their time. Fights can erupt over the amount of time each person spends taking care of children and managing their activities.

As children grow older, disagreements can erupt about discipline, education, house rules, and life expectations.

5. Chores

According to a Pew Research Center survey* of American adults, sharing household chores ranks third in importance on a list of nine items often associated with successful marriages—well ahead of adequate income, good housing, common interests, and shared religious beliefs.

Differing expectations, feelings about gender roles, and our early role models can cause friction related to divvying up the household chores. We also have a natural tendency to put more value on the work *we* do around the house and minimize the work our partners do. These conflicts about division of labor can mask deeper feelings related to respect, fairness, appreciation, and love.

6. Work

In the United States, 66 percent of married couples are dual income. In Canada, the percentage of husband-wife families that were dual earners is roughly 70 percent, and approximately two thirds of two-adult families have two incomes in the United Kingdom.

Managing a two-career relationship can add stress to your marriage and create a multitude of reasons for conflict, such as negotiating childcare and dividing chores.

It requires a series of tradeoffs between career growth, job demands, and commitments to your partner and kids. Couples can struggle with these tradeoffs, not only between work and personal life, but also between the perceived value of their individual careers related to their partner's career.

Even with couples where one partner works and the other stays at home, conflict can arise over the time the working partner is on the job, or the sense that the stay-at-home partner's contribution is devalued.

There are certainly other areas in which couples have conflict. I will cover twenty-one areas, including these six, in the letter writing templates.

Let's move on to some behaviors that immediately shut down verbal communication between a couple—situations that could signal it's time to write it out, rather than fight it out.

Barrie Davenport

Communication Killers That Make Talking Impossible

If you agree that healthy communication is a foundational piece of a happy relationship, then it's useful to know the kind of communication that is unhealthy and harmful—the kind that makes talking a destructive endeavor and letter writing a better option.

In your own relationship, you've experienced times when you've felt completely shut down, angered, or wounded by something your partner has said. More than likely, you've said a thing or two that has had the same effect on your partner.

We all do this. Sometimes it's unconscious and automatic, and other times it may well be calculated and intentional in order to get your partner's attention or to make him or her feel bad.

But if the goal here is to improve your communication so that you can enjoy a happier, more fulfilling life together, then you need to shine the light on anything that doesn't serve that purpose.

Words are powerful, and spoken in just the right combination and with just the right tone, you have the ability to enhance your intimacy or erode it. Rather than allowing words and tones to undermine your relationship, you can apply the brakes when you realize you or your partner are engaging in destructive communication.

This is a good time to step away from talk and turn to writing, once you both calm down and reflect. If you and your partner have developed a habit of using negative, toxic communication, you must stop these patterns as quickly as possible, if you want your relationship to thrive or even survive.

Dr. Gottman has gained powerful insights from studying couples who thrive (he calls them "Masters") and couples who don't (he calls them "Disasters").

In his book, *The Seven Principles for Making Marriage Work,* he outlines four types of negative communication that are lethal to a relationship. He calls them the "Four Horsemen of the Apocalypse."

Gottman has learned through his research with thousands of couples that if these four horsemen are allowed to run rampant in your communication, your relationship simply won't survive.

Here are the four most destructive ways you can communicate in your relationship. Do you and your partner engage in any of these on a regular basis?

#1: Criticism

When you criticize your partner, you are basically suggesting that their personality or character is the problem. The problem isn't the problem—your partner is the problem.

If you say something like, "Why don't you ever take the trash out? You are so lazy," then your wish to have the trash taken out becomes an indictment of your partner's character, rather than a complaint about behavior.

Complaining about a problem or a need is perfectly acceptable, but criticizing your partner isn't. Criticism is wounding, even if there is some truth to it—maybe especially so. It does nothing to affect the kind of positive change you are looking for.

As Dr. Gottman points out, those who are healthy communicators avoid criticism. He says,

> *"The Masters did the opposite: they point a finger at themselves and they really have a very gentle way of starting up the discussion, minimizing the problem and talking about what they feel and what they need."**

If criticism seems to rear its ugly head when you and your partner attempt to talk through an issue, use it as a warning sign to stop talking and start writing instead. The partner who is on the receiving end of the criticism may need to be the initiator here, as the critic may not be in the frame of mind to halt the discussion.

Try not to engage in a secondary argument about the criticism, but instead, step away, take some deep breaths, and return to the key points you want to make about the matter at hand so you can write down your thoughts. You can also address the criticism in writing, but don't allow it to escalate verbally.

#2: Contempt

Contempt is one of the most disrespectful ways you can communicate with your spouse or partner. It reveals your feelings of superiority over your partner—as though you are looking down on him or her and their character or personality.

Contempt shows up as sneering, sarcasm, cynicism, eye-rolling, name-calling, mockery, and hostile humor. It is a passive-aggressive way of expressing your inner feelings.

When you use these forms of verbal and non-verbal communication, you are showing disgust for your partner—the person you are supposed to love and cherish above all.

According to Dr. Gottman, "Contempt is fueled by long-simmering negative thoughts about the partner."* When you don't resolve the issues causing the negative thoughts, they creep out in condescending, derisive words that make your partner feel insulted and disrespected.

Dr. Gottman says that contempt not only predicts the breakup of relationships, but also,

> *"it predicted the number of infectious illnesses that the recipient of contempt would have in the next four years when we measured health."**

Contemptuous remarks are so profoundly hurtful that they have the power to make your partner physically ill.

Do you find yourself resorting to contempt when you communicate with your partner? If this has become a bad habit for you or your partner, and you can't immediately break the habit, then don't engage in the conflicts that trigger these reactions.

Spend some time thinking about situations that evoke contemptuous remarks from either of you. Rather than initiating a discussion about these hot-button topics, use letter writing instead. With letter writing, the reader can't see contemptuous facial expressions, but be careful not to allow contemptuous, sarcastic words to creep into your letter.

#3: Defensiveness

Defensiveness in conversation takes two forms—counterattacking or acting like an innocent victim and whining. Either way, it's a form of deflecting blame from yourself and putting it back onto your partner.

When we try to defend ourselves in a conflict, our defense rarely diffuses the situation or makes our partner feel heard and understood. It usually has the opposite effect, by escalating the conflict and further entrenching our partner's stance on the situation.

Imagine a scenario in which you tell your partner that his behavior is hurting you. Your partner immediately defends himself by saying, "Well, you do the same thing all the time!" This incites you to defend yourself, creating a circular argument that just intensifies your hurt feelings.

No one likes to have their bad behavior pointed out, but throwing out a defensive remark or acting like a victim when your partner has a complaint is not an emotionally mature response. It shows that you're more interested in being right than in finding a solution or healing a wound.

Defensiveness is such a common reaction in conflict that we often don't realize we're engaging in it. It becomes the go-to response when we feel insecure or threatened. But if you and your partner want to reach a harmonious resolution or decision, you need to drop it from all communication.

Start to pay attention to the ways defensiveness finds its way into your discussions. If you and your partner begin to bristle and put up walls when you talk, then end the conversation, and write your thoughts and feelings instead.

#4. Stonewalling

When you stonewall in communication, you shut down and tune out, essentially sending the message to your partner, "I don't care enough to engage with you." With stonewalling, you avoid responding altogether, or you respond in monosyllables or curt replies. It is often a response or reaction to ongoing criticism, contempt, and defensiveness between the two of you.

Let's say your partner brings up an issue she wants to discuss, but you stare at your smartphone without making eye contact or acknowledging her efforts to talk to you. You might say something like, "Do whatever you want," or "I don't have anything to say." This leaves your partner feeling frustrated, humiliated, and isolated.

According to research,* men tend to stonewall more than women, and they use this negative tactic when they feel overwhelmed by conflict. They just shut down in order to protect themselves from strong emotions or from feeling inadequate.

If stonewalling is a common communication tactic in your relationship, the stonewaller needs to realize how hurtful the behavior is to his or her partner. When it feels overwhelming to respond to your partner or spouse, acknowledge that you heard what was said, and step away from the conversation so you can put your thoughts and feelings in writing instead.

Every couple engages in these four horsemen tactics (criticism, contempt, defensiveness, and stonewalling) from time to time. It's human nature to feel defensive and critical on occasion. There are situations when your partner might behave in a way that makes you feel superior. In the heat of conflict, we all want to shut down and run away at times.

The problem occurs when these forms of communication become more the norm than the exception. If your relationship is characterized by these four horsemen, then you both need to sit up and take notice.

Eventually, you will need to learn to talk without these horsemen showing up in your conversations. But for now, you can prevent further damage by using another form of communication to express yourself without falling into these traps. Letter writing allows you to slow down, reflect, and edit your words, so you don't cause hurt feelings and anger.

Anger is another trap that can undermine your connection with your partner. It's hard not to feel angry when you've been hurt or disrespected, but anger can serve a positive purpose for healthy communication, as you will see in the next chapter.

Using Anger as a Warning

How many of your verbal conflicts with your partner have led to one or both of you becoming angry? It's a normal response in the heat of the moment, but anger can quickly erode your mutual affection, trust, and motivation to find solutions.

Quite often, we say and do things in anger that we later regret, things that make us look petty and small and that cause a deep rift in our intimacy with our partner.

Anger between you and your partner can also be damaging to your children. It's profoundly upsetting and frightening to them. Young children can believe they are the cause of their parents' anger, piling guilt feelings on top of their fears.

Expressing your anger is a release and can temporarily make you feel better, but it doesn't do much to help your relationship. In fact, despite claims to the contrary, research* has proven that venting your anger only makes you angrier. As a result, you have to spend time dealing with the fallout from your angry reactions that could be spent dealing with the real issue at hand.

Unfortunately, you can't just stop yourself from feeling anger. Something your partner says or does or neglects to do can trigger a flood of intense feelings. You can no more ignore these feelings than you can stop a steaming locomotive racing down the tracks.

The Purpose of Anger

As corrosive as it can be, anger does serve a purpose in exposing the seriousness of the issue you and your partner are facing. Your anger reflects myriad feelings that have been simmering beneath the surface that need to be addressed. Anger energizes you to respond and take action.

You've likely learned the hard way that responding while angry isn't the smartest idea. The best thing anger can do for you in the midst of a conflict with your partner is to serve as a big, flashing stop sign. Once you realize you are angry, use whatever remains of your rational mind to take a few deep breaths, count to ten, and excuse yourself from the conversation.

Of course, you need to recognize when you are angry, before you can step away and calm down. Some of us push down angry feelings or try to manage them until they surprise us by bursting out in a tirade.

Sometimes anger is mild or moderate but can still cause an undercurrent of discord between you and your partner. Either way, there are definite signs and bodily changes that accompany anger.

- Adrenaline and other chemicals begin to surge through your body.

- Your heart rate speeds up, which prepares you for aggressive action.

- You may begin to finger point to emphasize your words or form a clenched fist to appear threatening.

- You either set your mouth in a firm closure to contain your angry feelings, or you start spouting harsh and critical words.

- Your voice becomes increasingly loud and fast.

- You become more focused on your partner's perceived bad behavior and lose the capacity to see your part of the problem.

- You don't want to hear anything that contradicts your angry beliefs. You are hyperfocused on yourself.

- The executive, functioning part of your brain, allowing you to analyze and solve problems, appears to shut down. You are in fight-or-flight mode, putting you at risk for aggression.

- The angrier you become, the more negatively you perceive the situation, as your senses are giving you unreliable data. You overgeneralize and see the other person as worse than they really are.

You can prevent your angry feelings from doing harm to your relationship by using them as a warning sign to the conversation. When you notice irritation setting in or signs of full-blown anger boiling over, pause and remove yourself from the situation. Step out of the room for a moment. Tell your partner you need a break to calm down.

Take some slow, deep breaths, focusing on your breathing, rather than your angry thoughts. Drink some cool water to cool yourself down. Do something distracting, such as folding laundry or cleaning out your car. Take enough time to allow your anger to dissipate, so that you can think more clearly.

Once you've calmed down, you need to look at yourself and the situation dispassionately. There are several things to consider before you begin writing your thoughts and feelings.

Think about—

- Determine possible risk factors for anger, like being tired, hungry, overwhelmed, premenstrual, or feeling ill. Anger is cumulative, so maybe something happened earlier in the day to trigger your anger more easily with your partner.

- Consider any possible miscommunications or misunderstandings that might have led to your irritated feelings.

- Ask yourself what role you played in the difficulty. For a moment, take the focus off your partner and look at yourself. Believe it or not, if you discover you played a larger role in the upset, you will feel calmer.

- Rather than focusing on what you want your partner to do, focus on what you want. For example, rather than demanding, "I want her to have dinner ready by 6:00," you might suggest, "I want to eat dinner earlier." This opens the door to finding solutions.

- Think about solutions that you yourself can take rather than focusing on what your partner needs to do.

Once you have time to process these thoughts and feel more clear-headed and calm, you can write a letter to your partner that focuses on the issue and the reasons behind your anger, rather than venting your anger and causing further damage.

Remember, the best way to prevent anger from undermining a constructive conflict is by heading it off at the pass. Don't indulge your anger when it arises. Pay attention to your feelings and use them as a warning to stop and step away.

Anger is destructive to your communication and your relationship. You can't always avoid feeling it, but you can avoid using it. If it seems anger is still too near the surface to return to a discussion, then write your thoughts and feelings instead.

A Word about Vulnerability

Once, when I was feeling particularly stressed and overwhelmed, my sister said, "Just fall back and let the universe catch you." As she said that, a feeling of peace washed over me. How lovely it would be to let go and feel completely safe, knowing that everything would be okay and that I was okay.

Imagine if you heard those words from your beloved, "Just fall back and let me catch you. Just fall back and tell me everything. Just fall back and be yourself, flaws and all. I will still love you. I will be there for you."

Imagine the peace of not holding it all in, of being completely authentic and open, sharing your most intimate dreams, deepest fears, and shameful feelings, perfectly secure in the knowledge you won't be ridiculed or rejected. Instead, you'll be embraced.

Unfortunately, most of us have been trained from an early age not to be vulnerable, not to share our weaknesses or fears. We've learned the painful lesson of opening our hearts, telling our truths, and showing our frailties, only to have our hearts broken and our weaknesses disparaged. We've learned to hold back, to pretend to be someone else, and to protect our hearts.

We've also learned that the best defense against pain is a good offense. So, we build brick walls. We hold ourselves at arm's length. Of course, it's exhausting and stressful, maintaining this pretense. It takes a lot of energy to be something you're not and keep your partner at arm's distance.

It does protect you from emotional pain in the short term, but in the long run, it wreaks havoc on your relationship. Without being vulnerable, intimacy will wither and die, like a flower that never develops deep roots.

In your relationship or marriage, this kind of openness should be the norm. But it requires that you regularly communicate your feelings with your partner, rather than hiding them or stuffing them. Eventually, with practice, it should become easier to be completely authentic with your partner, if you feel safe and accepted.

Vulnerability requires letting down your guard and inviting your partner into your inner world. Your ability to be vulnerable and to communicate freely with your partner is essential for intimacy in your relationship. Why? For many reasons.

Vulnerability reveals the complete person you are.

When you are able to show yourself fully to another person, you experience the joy of being fully yourself. And he or she benefits from knowing all of you, not just the glossed-over, surface level parts of you.

You both enjoy the depths and complexities of all aspects of each other—the good, the bad, and the ugly. There is beauty and healing in being known so completely.

Vulnerability also fosters trust.

As you reveal yourself to your partner, and he or she responds with respect, love, and dignity, your trust in your partner expands. As you open up and share more of yourself, you also invite your partner to be vulnerable.

You give your partner the courage to show his or her hidden or shameful feelings. Both of you experience the security and peace of having the other's back and knowing you are still loved and respected.

Being vulnerable with each other invites growth.

It allows you to honestly reflect on your true self within the safe harbor of a trusting relationship. You can assess changes you need to make and the person you want to become, without taking a blow to your self-esteem.

Self-honesty is critical to living authentically, which in turn opens doors to untapped potential within yourself.

Vulnerable sharing builds your confidence.

As you express your feelings, revealing your flaws, and admitting your fears, you see that the practice of vulnerability actually strengthens you.

You realize you can expose yourself without dying or becoming less of a person. You are bolstered by your ability to stand firm in your own truth.

Vulnerability heals wounds.

All healing begins with acknowledgment, acceptance, and awareness. When you are real about your pain or fear, rather than trying to run from it or hide it, you purge yourself of the blocked feelings and stress of trying to pretend or ignore.

By putting things out in the open with your partner, you allow the light of truth to ignite the healing process.

Vulnerability creates bonds.

All of us have areas of ourselves we fear revealing or sharing with another person, even our partner or spouse. We all have pain, shameful feelings, and self-doubt. When you're able to open up about these with the most important person in your life, you connect even more deeply with *their* humanness. You allow them to see that you are just like them, that you share common feelings and concerns. This bonds you closer to each other.

Sharing in a vulnerable way deepens your love.

Vulnerability means you are able to express your deepest feelings and share love on a more profound level. You can be completely open emotionally, mentally, and physically, and embrace that same openness from your loved one without fear of rejection.

Vulnerability makes us more attractive and interesting.

Nothing is more appealing than authenticity. By being fully yourself, and confidently accepting your good and bad qualities, you become more interesting and attractive. Your ability to express yourself openly and acknowledge your flaws makes your partner also feel safe and confident around you.

Vulnerability teaches us comfort with uncertainty.

When we are vulnerable, we don't always know how our partner will respond to us. We take a huge risk by putting ourselves out there. This uncertainty causes discomfort and tension.

But by practicing vulnerable sharing, you grow accustomed to uncertainty and can tolerate the unpleasant feelings it causes. You can use this new toughness to cope with other areas of risk in your life that can stretch you and expand opportunities for growth.

Is Vulnerability Uncomfortable for You?

For many of you reading this book, expressing and sharing your vulnerabilities verbally can be deeply uncomfortable. You may desire an intimate, open relationship with your spouse or partner, but you just can't say the words out loud.

You have a hard time verbalizing the deeper feelings, fears, and insecurities behind your reactions and behaviors. You might feel embarrassed or ashamed of your feelings, even though you'd like to be open with your partner.

If this is the case, rather than shutting your partner out, letter writing can be a safer, less uncomfortable way to invite intimacy and vulnerability. During verbal conflict, we tend to build walls around ourselves to keep at arm's distance from our partner, so we don't have to experience more pain. With letter writing, we don't feel as exposed, so it's easier to let down the walls and reveal our true selves without defensiveness or anger.

As bestselling author and vulnerability expert Brené Brown reminds us in *The Gifts of Imperfection*,

> *"Owning our story can be hard but not nearly as difficult as spending our lives running from it. Embracing our vulnerabilities is risky but not nearly as dangerous as giving up on love and belonging and joy—the experiences that make us the most vulnerable. Only when we are brave enough to explore the darkness will we discover the infinite power of our light."**

Don't allow your fears, insecurities, and discomfort to prevent you from developing an emotionally intimate, vulnerable, authentic relationship with your partner. If you can't say it with words, write it on paper. The more you practice and realize your written words are respected by your partner, the more comfortable you'll become with being vulnerable and even speaking your truth.

How to Use These Letter Writing Templates

We've established that talking can be hard for couples, especially during conflict and about difficult or sensitive topics. But writing can be tricky too, if you don't start with some ground rules and clear objectives.

The main goal here is for letter writing to be a positive, healing experience for you and your partner—not just another way of getting your point across, avoiding conflict, or making a dig. Your letters should be a way of expressing yourself in a mature, thoughtful, and kind way when words fail you.

Remember, your spoken words can be forgotten or misremembered, but when you put something in writing, it can last forever. Your partner might read your letter over and over again to refresh his or her memory or to savor your words. It is a permanent record of your thoughts and feelings, so you want to reflect your best self in writing. Never write anything you will later regret.

I've written these templates related to a number of situations that typically trigger conflict or difficult conversations for couples. There's no way to anticipate the *exact* issues you and your partner will experience together, so I have created different scenarios for each of the topics that you can use as templates for your own unique issues. Many of your conflicts and discussions will likely fall into these categories.

The scripts are intended to help you craft phrases and use appropriate words for more loving, intentional, and healing written communication. You can pull sentences or ideas and rephrase them, or use them in your own way that best suits the issue at hand.

All of these letters follow some basic guidelines to ensure you are improving your communication skills and enhancing your relationship.

Here are some parameters to consider before you get started:

Write when you are calm and collected.

Your writing should be done thoughtfully, kindly, and in the spirit of love. If you are still too angry or wounded to write from this loving position, then wait before you write—and definitely wait before you give your partner the letter.

Know your goal.

What do you want to achieve with your letter? Is it to explain yourself more calmly? Ask for a behavior change? Offer an apology? Share something vulnerable? Suggest a solution? Open the door to a conversation?

Have a specific goal in mind, and try not to cover too many objectives with one letter. Give your partner, as the reader, something firm to focus on and deal with. You can always write more, once you resolve or clarify the first topic or issue.

Also, if you need or expect a response back from your partner, ask for it directly, and let your partner know if you'd like the response in writing, especially if you think you're not ready to talk.

Handwriting is better than email, text, or typing.

A handwritten letter forces you to process your thoughts slowly and deliberately. It is more personal and caring and shows you took the time to consider your words.

If the information is sensitive, handwriting (rather than email) also minimizes the possibility that your words will be seen by the wrong people. Never text your thoughts about a conflict or serious topic. It is not the right forum for serious, meaningful communication.

If you have children in the house, and you don't want them to see your letter, be sure to put it in a sealed envelope and privately give it to your spouse or partner.

Begin with positives.

Set the stage for your partner to receive your words well by beginning with loving, affirmative words. You might begin with, "I love you so much, and I really want to work this out," or "Our relationship is so important to me, and I hope you'll read my words in the loving way they are intended."

This reduces the chance your partner will feel defensive or upset before you have a chance to communicate your thoughts and feelings later in the letter.

Focus on your own feelings rather than your partner's behaviors.

Try to use the words, "I feel," rather than "You are," or "You make me . . ."

For example, you might say, "I feel disrespected when you cut me off," rather than, "You are so rude and thoughtless when you interrupt me."

During conflict, it is usually the *feelings* the situation fosters that need to be identified, acknowledged, and addressed before a change or solution can be agreed on.

The ability to identify and communicate your own feelings is an essential part of this conflict resolution strategy. Beginning with the words, "I feel," can help you examine and express your feelings.

Be direct and forthright in a kind way.

Rather than hinting about what you want or assuming your partner will intuit it, state it clearly without being unkind or thoughtless—for example, "I want you to hug me more often every day."

State your desires in the positive—what you want, rather than what you don't want. Rather than saying, "I don't want you hanging out with your friends so much," say, "I would like to spend more time with you."

Being direct doesn't mean you should tell off your partner or give him or her a piece of your mind. It means being clear about what you want or need in the relationship, even if it's uncomfortable for your partner.

Being direct and forthright, especially if you fear hurting or angering your partner, can be hard during conversation. But in writing, you are able to state things succinctly without the anxiety that often holds you back in face-to-face conversation.

Use the word "and" rather than "but."

Using the word "but" when explaining your position can have a nullifying effect, even if it is prefaced by a positive phrase. It tends to brush aside your partner's feelings or opinion in order to minimize or invalidate them.

For example, if you write, "I understand why you want to go on the vacation, **but** I think we can't afford it," then you have essentially shut down your partner's feelings.

Instead, try something like, "I understand why you want to go on vacation, **and** I really want to go too. I also feel uncomfortable about the expense."

The word "and" shows that there is more than one way to perceive the situation without diminishing your partner's position when you happen to have a different position.

Edit your words carefully.

The beauty of putting it in writing is that you have the time to think about what you want to say, and time to make sure your words won't intentionally trigger anger or pain for your partner.

You know your partner well enough to know what will hurt or offend him or her, and this letter writing technique is counterproductive, if you fall back on those harmful words. Don't use any subtle digs, offhand criticism, blaming, shaming, or defensive language in a letter that is meant to enhance communication and healing.

Read your letter carefully before you give it to your partner, and try to read it from his or her perspective. Change any language that could be misunderstood or misinterpreted.

If an apology is in order, do it first.

If you need to apologize for your words or behavior, do that at the beginning of the letter. Don't try to minimize or hide your apology by burying it, after you defend or explain yourself.

When you apologize, offer a full and complete apology. Begin your letter with something like this: "I am so sorry that I yelled at you like I did. That was inexcusable and hurtful, and I promise I won't do it again. I hope you'll forgive me."

Own your behavior, promise to change it, and ask for forgiveness. And be sure to follow through on changing the behavior.

Stay on point and use concise language.

Your letter doesn't need to be a novel. It doesn't need flowery language or complex words. Write as though you are speaking, using your authentic voice and personal language. The templates in this book will present ideas and phrases you can use, but if a word strikes you as something you'd never say, by all means, change it.

Say enough to reach your goal with the letter, but not so much that your partner becomes confused or overwhelmed. This is especially important with sensitive, difficult issues that trigger a lot of emotion.

Think about how it feels when a doctor gives you an unpleasant diagnosis, followed by a litany of explanations and next steps. You feel overwhelmed and can't focus on the flood of information. Presentation can make a huge difference in how your words are understood and accepted by your partner.

It may take several letters with your partner for particularly sticky or difficult topics, just as it often takes many discussions to work through a conflict. It is better for both of you to take it slowly and unravel the issue one step at a time.

Think about your presentation.

Before you hand over your letter to your partner, consider how he or she is feeling and how receptive they will be to your letter. If it's clear your partner is still angry, or he or she is distracted, tight on time, or otherwise not available to read the letter with full attention and a clear head, then wait to offer it.

Also, determine if you want to be with your partner when he or she reads it. You may want to sit with your partner while he or she is reading so you can be available to answer questions or begin a discussion based on your letter.

You may decide to be away from the house entirely to give your partner a chance to process your words, especially if you suspect he or she will react badly, no matter how well you presented your feelings in the letter.

Consider reading your letter out loud.

Letter writing helps you gather your thoughts and express them without the intense emotion that makes thinking (and talking) on your feet so difficult. You may really wish you could talk with your partner about your feelings, but you get emotional or tongue-tied when you do.

If this is the case for you, then write your thoughts in the form of a letter, and read it out loud to your partner. Explain why you need to do this, and once you read it out loud, allow your partner to read the letter again silently. This practice can break the ice and open the door to a more productive conversation.

Even if you decide not to read it out loud to your partner, it's helpful on many levels to read it out loud to yourself. First, hearing yourself speak the words can help you determine if you've chosen them wisely. Once you say them out loud, they may sound curt, sarcastic, or unkind, which is not your intention.

Also, reading the letter out loud reinforces a more positive communication style in your memory. If you write the letter in an emotionally mature and thoughtful way, then you mentally bolster this language and can more easily recall it in later conversations. Ultimately, you want to be able to communicate verbally without difficulty.

For the sake of convenience with these letters, I use the names of the fictitious couple I referenced at the beginning of the book—Sarah and Jason.

However, these templates are intended for any couple in an intimate, committed relationship who are living together, whether they are straight or gay.

What to Do If Your Partner Responds Badly

I mentioned earlier the importance of reading this book with your spouse or partner, or at least telling your partner about the ideas presented here to invite participation. Whether it's talking or letter writing, healthy communication involves two people with similar motivations and desires for improving the relationship.

It's often the case that one partner will pick up a relationship book, sign up for a course, or initiate a meeting with a therapist in order to find solutions to relationship problems. But the other partner shows no interest or willingness to participate.

The unwilling partner might feel too threatened, embarrassed, or uncomfortable to face the problems in the relationship and deal with them. He or she might be in denial about the issues you are having with the relationship, thinking they aren't big enough to merit "working" on them.

Your partner might have low self-esteem or insecurities that make any attempt at relationship repair seem like an indictment of his or her character. Sometimes one partner is emotionally unavailable, too prideful, or simply disinterested in doing the work to improve the relationship.

Hitting these roadblocks with your partner, especially when you are trying earnestly to communicate with love and kindness, can feel devastating. If your partner doesn't participate or responds to your letters defensively or with anger, you feel like you have hit a stalemate. How can you ever work through your issues to rebuild your intimacy, trust, and happiness?

If your partner refuses to participate in responding to your letters, or if he or she responds (either verbally or in writing) with anger, contempt, sarcasm, criticism, or defensiveness, here are a few options to consider.

Give it some time.

Just as we often respond verbally without thinking, your partner might read a letter and dash off a response without considering the words. Don't respond to a defensive, unkind letter from your partner. Just wait a day or two to see if he or she comes around. Your silence might invite a more considered response, after the initial feelings of anger or hurt have faded.

Write another letter.

Focus the letter on how your partner's negative response made you feel and your sincere hope that you can work out your problem without hurting each other. Ask your partner for another response that is more thoughtful and healing. Hopefully he or she will soften to your sincere reply.

Ask to meet with a couple's counselor.

If neither verbal nor written communication is working, and your partner is unwilling or unable to communicate kindly and maturely, then you may need the support of a professional. Ask your partner to join you for couple's counseling, and let him or her know how imperative this is for the health of your relationship.

Take your letters with you to the session, as they can be useful in giving the counselor a window into your communication problems.

Meet with a counselor by yourself.

If your partner refuses couple's counseling, go on your own. Talk to the counselor about your attempts at communicating verbally and in writing and how your partner has responded. The counselor might have other strategies to help you invite your partner to join in the sessions.

Even if he or she won't join you, sometimes the best way to help your partner is to model positive change in yourself. One partner making a major change in a relationship can change the entire relationship.

As you learn better communication skills yourself, you can encourage your partner to communicate better. You can teach your partner to respect you by respecting him or her. You can show your partner a new way to respond by speaking or writing with love and kindness consistently.

Some Final Instructions

Here are some final points to consider as you review these letter templates.

- Review these scripts when you are in a positive, calm frame of mind. If you are feeling

73

hurt or angry at your partner, the words in these templates won't feel true for you. You may find yourself resisting them.

- Read through all the scripts before you write your own letter, as you may decide to pull language from one topic to use with another.

- As you read the scripts, think about any issues you and your partner are experiencing or topics you need to discuss.

- Have a journal and pen handy to write down sentences, phrases, and words you would like to use in your letter or letters.

- If other words or ideas are triggered for you as you read these scripts, write those down also.

- Tell your partner that you are reading this book and why you want to try letter writing in certain situations. Don't surprise your partner with a series of letters, if this is a new way of communicating for the two of you.

Are you ready to get started? Let's move on to the twenty-one relationship topics where I offer four letter writing examples for each topic.

84 Letter Writing Templates

Section 1
Unloving Words and Behaviors

Letter #1: I am hurt by your words.

Dear Sarah,

There is no one in the world who means more to me than you. And there's no one whose good opinion of me counts more than yours.

That's why I am so stung by what you said to me this morning. Your words are powerful, and I felt so hurt and misunderstood when you called me a selfish bastard. I didn't deserve that.

I hope that you don't really see me that way and that you just let the words fly without thinking.

I know you were upset and angry, and I understand that. I also know there is a better way to share your feelings without attacking me or calling me names.

I'm asking that you never say that again to me, even in jest. I need you to speak kindlier to me and consider the impact of your words before you say them.

Will you write me back and let me know if you can agree to this?

Love,
Jason

Letter #2: I need you to stop dismissing my opinion.

Dear Jason,

You are the smartest man I know and so knowledgeable in many areas. That's one of the reasons I fell in love with you and respect you so much.

I'm writing to request that same respect from you. Let me explain.

The other night when we were discussing the movie we saw and what we thought about it, you made some great points. I had some thoughts I wanted to share too and was excited to talk with you about them.

When I started to share my opinion, you cut me off and told me I was wrong. It felt like you didn't care about my opinion or respect my intellect. It really deflated me and sapped the fun from our date night.

It seems that you frequently talk over me and dismiss my opinions, and it really hurts. I am especially sensitive about it because my dad always did this, and it made me feel so small and stupid.

It triggers those same feelings when you dismiss me and my ideas. I need to know you are respectful of my thoughts and opinions and want to hear what I have to say.

I need you to listen more to me without cutting me off, to acknowledge my opinions, and to show more interest when I'm talking.

Are you willing to do that? Please respond to this letter and let me know your thoughts.

Love,
Sarah

Letter #3: Your constant criticism makes me feel unappreciated.

Dear Sarah,

When we were first dating, I remember overhearing you tell your mom that I was the perfect guy for you, and that you couldn't think of anything I did wrong.

I felt so happy when I heard that, because even though I know I'm not perfect, I wanted to be perfect for you and make you happy.

During the past few months, it seems you are unhappy with me and that there's not much I'm doing right in your eyes. When you criticized me this morning, saying that I always leave the messy kitchen for you to clean up, I felt so unappreciated. If you think about it, you know I clean up all the time.

This kind of criticism has happened several times recently, where you've told me I "always" do something I shouldn't do or "never" do things I should. Last week it was about mowing the lawn and before that you criticized the way I handled the vacation plans.

Write It Out, Don't Fight It Out

When you do this, it makes me feel really dishonored and frustrated. I want to feel that you love and appreciate me, just as I love and appreciate you.

I know there are ways I could step up more, and I also know I work hard to be a good husband and parent.

I would like you to try harder to focus on the good things I do, rather than the things that bother you, and try to remember that guy you found so perfect at the beginning. :)

If you have a concern about something I do, please don't criticize me or make sweeping remarks about my actions. Just tell me nicely what's bothering you, and we can work it out.

I love you and hope you accept my request. You can write me back if you want.

Love,
Jason

Letter #4: I feel shut out when you give the silent treatment.

Dear Jason,

I feel really bad about our argument and hate it when we are angry at each other. I love you so much and don't want this distance between us.

I really wanted to work things out last night and hoped you'd be willing to talk about the problem. Then you just closed down and stopped talking completely.

I want you to know how it impacts me when you do that. When you refuse to talk or even tell me why you won't talk, I feel so rejected and shut out. It gives me so much anxiety, because it triggers the way I felt when Dad started giving us the silent treatment right before he left Mom.

I understand if you feel too overwhelmed or frustrated to talk in the heat of the moment, and I hope you understand how much it hurts me when you don't give me something to indicate we're going to work this out.

We need to keep communicating somehow so we don't pull apart. Is it possible for you to say enough to make me feel connected to you and not pushed away?

I want to understand you better and what happens when you shut down like this. Will you please write back and tell me what is on your mind about the argument and why you couldn't talk last night?

I love you and want us to work this out.

Love,
Sarah

Section 2
Power Struggles

Letter #5: It feels competitive when you tell me how to cook.

Dear Sarah,

You are an amazing cook and meal planner. The dinner you made for our guests last week was fantastic. I have always been so proud of your skills in the kitchen.

I know I'm not the chef that you are. Still I enjoy cooking and coming up with ideas for dinner. I find it relaxing and fun to make dinner a few times a week.

When I'm in the kitchen cooking, you often come in to tell me how to do things or how I could make the meal better. It feels like we're in a competition for who makes the best dinner, and that you can't be happy with the way I do things.

I don't want to feel like I'm being instructed or judged while I'm making dinner. I just want to enjoy cooking and serving dinner to you—and to have you enjoy and appreciate it without making suggestions.

We are partners, and even though I know you are the more skilled cook, I need your appreciation and positive feedback when I prepare the meal without instruction or criticism.

Will you honor this request?

Love,
Jason

Letter #6: I feel disrespected when you make decisions without me.

Dear Jason,

I was thinking today about how much fun it was when we were house hunting for our first home.

We were really a team, finding a great deal in the neighborhood we wanted, negotiating the contract, and then fixing up the house together. This is one of my favorite memories of our time together.

Since then, it seems we've fallen into a pattern that isn't teamwork anymore. You have made some important decisions without my input or approval during the past year, the most recent being the purchase of the new car.

It's been bothering me more and more, and I need for things to change.

When you make a decision that impacts both of us without consulting me, it feels disrespectful, like you don't see me as an equal partner. We are in this relationship together, and it is important for both of us that I'm equally invested in all these important decisions.

From now on, I want us to discuss all decisions that impact us both, even the small ones. I know this will

83

bring us closer, and it will make me feel more respected by you.

Please respond to this letter, and let me know your thoughts.

Love,
Sarah

Letter #7: I feel manipulated when you sulk if things don't go your way.

Dear Sarah,

Making you happy is one of the greatest joys of my life. I love seeing your beautiful smile.

There are many times when I'm happy to go along with your decision on something, even if it wouldn't be my first choice. There are other times when I really don't want to do something, or I want something different.

When you sulk and withdraw from me during those situations, it feels like you are intentionally trying to make me feel bad and that you see your needs as more important than mine.

It seems you use sulking as a way to let me know you're displeased with me, so that I will give in and do things your way. I feel disrespected and manipulated when you do that, and it puts me in the position of having to defend my opinions.

Both of us deserve the freedom and safety to say no if we don't want to do something, without the other sulking or pulling away. I need to feel that you still love and respect me, even if I don't agree with everything you want or need. I'm always happy to talk things through or work out a compromise.

I am asking you from now on to accept my wishes or ask for a compromise without sulking, giving me the cold shoulder, or getting irritated with me. Are you willing to do that?

Please let me know your thoughts.

Love,
Jason

Letter #8: I feel threatened by your promotion.

Dear Jason,

I can't tell you how proud I am of you. You so deserved this promotion, and I know you are going to be an amazing manager.

I don't want to burst our happiness bubble about this big event. I am really excited about the pay raise and what that means for our family. I'm also feeling a little threatened and fearful about the changes this job will bring.

As your career is taking off, I'm seeing how mine is receding in the distance now that I'm home with the kids full-time. I'm worried that you won't see me as an equal partner or view my opinions as relevant anymore. I guess I'm also a little resentful that I'm missing out on "real" life in the working world.

Now that you'll be traveling more, I wonder if you will "grow past" me, since you'll meet so many new people and have interesting travel and work experiences while I'm at home with the children. Your busier schedule means I'll have to be even more hands-on with them.

I need to still feel engaged in life and the working world, even though I spend most of my time raising the kids. I need this so that you and I stay connected and so that I feel better about myself.

We are both committed to me staying home while the kids are young. Still, I'd like to figure out a way to keep my foot in the door with my career so I don't feel so cut off from you and the work I enjoyed for so long. I'd like your thoughts (and reassurance) about this.

When would be a good time for us to talk about this? I'd suggest Sunday night after the kids are in bed.

Love,
Sarah

Section 3
Unrealistic Expectations

Letter #9: I can't read your mind.

Dear Sarah,

I love you, and I feel so sad about how we left things last night. It was not my intention to upset you.

When we talked about me having dinner with the guys earlier in the week, you encouraged me to go. You didn't say anything about needing me home early to help with the kids.

You said last night that I should have known that you would need me home early. I didn't get that impression at all from you earlier in the week when we talked about it.

I sometimes get mixed messages from you, and I feel confused and frustrated when you tell me to take time for myself and then get mad at me later. I can't read your mind, if you don't tell me what you really want or need.

That doesn't mean I don't love you. It just means I don't always know what you are thinking. I feel like I'm walking on eggshells sometimes, because I don't know what will or won't upset you. I don't like that feeling.

We both need time for ourselves—we've agreed on that. I need for you to accept that I can't know what you are thinking, unless you tell me specifically, even if you think I should know.

From now on, will you please tell me directly any specific expectations you have so we can discuss them beforehand? Please respond and let me know your thoughts.

Love,
Jason

Letter #10: My priorities aren't always your priorities.

Dear Jason,

You and I have always marveled at how compatible we are and how much we have in common. It's one of the things I most love about us.

I could tell how hurt you were this morning when I said I didn't want to spend the weekend planting the garden with you. I know you've spent a lot of time planning this and getting excited about it.

As much as I love you and want to share things with you, working outside and planting is just not my thing. Weekends are precious for both of us, and I just wouldn't enjoy spending this one planting.

As compatible as we are, we won't always have the same priorities. I hope you can respect my priorities, when they are different from yours, without getting upset. I need to feel free to be honest with you and know that you won't get mad.

Please let me know if you understand and agree to what I'm asking here. Let's try to find something we can both enjoy doing together for part of the weekend, even if we don't plant together.

Love,
Sarah

Letter #11: I feel rejected when you don't accept who I am.

Dear Sarah,

Do you remember during our first date when you said you found quiet guys more interesting? I was so relieved when you said that, because I was afraid you would think I was boring.

I'm worried now that your feelings have changed. I am still the same person I was when we met. Yes, I am reserved, and I'm not going to be the life of the party.

When you made that sarcastic comment about it last night in front of our friends, I felt humiliated and rejected by you. It feels like you want me to change to be someone else and that you don't love me as I am.

I have made an effort to be more sociable and talkative, because I know it makes you happy. I need you to try harder to accept my personality without getting frustrated or making hurtful remarks.

Your love and acceptance of me are what I value most in this world. Can you accept me as I am?

Love,
Jason

Letter #12: I can't always agree with you.

Dear Jason,

I hope you will read this letter in the spirit of love and goodwill it's intended.

I respect your opinions and beliefs wholeheartedly. I just can't always agree with them.

I know you wanted me to back you up with your parents last night in your disagreement with them, and I understand you were angry when I didn't say anything.

The truth is, I don't share your assessment of the situation with them. I didn't say anything because I didn't want to openly disagree with you in front of your parents. However, I couldn't tell a lie either.

I have my own perspective about things and being married doesn't mean we will always share the same perspectives. I know you don't always share my assessment of things or my opinions, and I accept that.

When you expect me to back you up or agree with your opinion, and then get angry if I don't, it feels like your love and kindness are conditional.

I don't deserve your anger when I disagree with you, and I'm asking if you will please respect my opinions more graciously.

Love,
Sarah

Section 4
Big Priority Differences

Letter #13: I'm not ready for kids.

Dear Sarah,

I know this is going to be a hard subject, and I want to start by saying how much I love you and want you to be happy.

You have made it clear how much you want children and how important it is for you to be a mom. I understand why you feel pressured to start trying because you turned 30 this year.

I believe it is important for both of us to feel ready and prepared to take on the responsibility of children before we start trying. I'm just not there yet. I want to be an engaged and hands-on dad. I need to feel settled with other things in our lives so I can be.

You want me to give you an exact date when I will be ready, and I'd like to do that. I just started this new job, we have some serious debt to pay off, and we talked about wanting to buy a house before getting pregnant.

Having a child this year is a priority for you. Right now, it isn't for me, and it makes me feel overwhelmed and anxious when you keep bringing it up. I know neither of us wants to enter parenthood feeling pressured by the other.

I love you, Sarah, and we will have children. I'm asking you to give me six months without pushing me about it, so I have enough time to process everything else in our lives. Then we can talk about it again. Are you agreeable to that?

Love,
Jason

Letter #14: I don't want to move.

Dear Jason,

I have always loved your spirit of adventure and willingness to try new things. You have made life so exciting and fun for our family.

I can see why this opportunity to move to San Francisco is so appealing. I love the city as much as you do. I don't relish shutting down this idea, because I know you are so excited about it. I just don't want to move.

I have a great network of friends here, and the kids are only a few miles away. They would have to drive eight hours to get to San Francisco. Plus, I love our house, and we've worked so hard to get it just like we want it.

When I think about leaving our home here, I feel sad and resistant. We had to move so many times when I was a kid, and I finally feel settled in a real home with good friends and family nearby.

How can we make this work so we both feel good about the decision? Maybe there's a way to spend more time in the city or spend part of the summer there. I am open to ideas.

Please write back and let me know what you think.

Love,
Sarah

Letter #15: I feel like we're moving in different directions.

Dear Sarah,

I love you and the life we have built together. I'm so proud of our family and what we've accomplished throughout the years.

Lately I've been feeling sad and concerned, because it seems we are drifting in different directions. As my work has slowed down, yours has picked up, and you have a new group of friends who I don't really know.

I have to admit, I feel left out when you go to your weekly pottery class, even though I'm glad you have found this creative outlet. This used to be our game night together with the kids, and I miss those fun evenings.

We've both gotten more comfortable doing our own things, and it's beginning to feel like we're living more as roommates than the close couple we use to be. I miss spending time with you and just talking. I miss the things we used to do together, like hiking and making dinners together. I really miss making love more than once every few months.

I'd like to know if you also feel this drift. If so, do you want to repair it and become close again? Is there something more that we need to address?

You are the love of my life, and I want us to find a way back to the couple we used to be. I don't want our differing interests and schedules to keep pulling us apart.

I have some ideas for bringing us closer, and I want to hear yours. I want to know if there's a deeper problem we need to work on.

Please write back and let me know how you feel about what I've shared and asked you in this letter.

Love,
Jason

Letter #16: I feel I prioritize our relationship more than you do.

Dear Jason,

Have I told you recently how important you are to me and how much our relationship means? You and this marriage are the most valuable things in my life.

Write It Out, Don't Fight It Out

I want us to have a strong and happy marriage, and for me, nothing else takes priority over that. Recently I've been feeling like I put more value on our relationship and how it's going than you do.

When you refuse to talk about issues between us, like you did last night, or when you choose to spend several nights out during the week with your friends, I feel hurt and unloved. It seems like you don't value me and our relationship enough to make an effort to work on it. This has been happening more and more, and it is creating a wall between us.

We need to be able to communicate and spend time together for our marriage to stay strong. I firmly believe a good relationship takes effort. I am more than willing to put in that effort, and I need to know you are too.

I'm asking that you spend only one night a week out with the guys, so that you and I can spend more time together. Also, I'd like for us to talk (or write) at least once a week about how our marriage is going and discuss any issues that come up so we can work them out.

Can you do this graciously, without feeling resentment? This is so important for me and our marriage, and I hope you will think about it with an open mind. Please write back and let me know what you think.

I love you,
Sarah

Section 5
Pet Peeves

Letter #17: Please stop talking with your mouth full.

Dear Sarah,

I love you, and I don't ever want to embarrass you.

I have something I want to bring to your attention that has been bothering me, and you may not be aware of it.

When you eat, you talk with your mouth full of food. You are such a classy woman, and I know you don't want to offend anyone with this.

I sure don't want to hurt you by pointing this out. It's something I just hope you will pay attention to.

I love you,
Jason

Letter #18: Please put the toilet seat down.

Dear Jason,

What will you do when your loving wife falls into the toilet and is never seen again? :)

We've talked about the toilet seat thing before, and I know it doesn't seem like a big deal to you. Here's why I need you to pay more attention to putting it down after you use it.

When I get up to go to the bathroom at night, I keep the light off, so I won't disturb you. I can't see if the seat is up or down, so I end up sitting on the exposed bowl, which is kind of gross and uncomfortable. I've fallen into the water a few times. Yuck.

Also, guests and other people in the house don't want to grab the seat to put it down or see any unsightly drips under the seat.

I'm trying to be a little humorous here, and I would really appreciate it if you'd be more mindful of putting the seat down. Will you agree to try this?

Love,
Sarah

Letter #19: I feel frustrated by your chronic tardiness.

Dear Sarah,

I'm sorry I got so irritated at you this morning. I overreacted, and I shouldn't have yelled at you. I love you and hope you'll forgive me for that.

I think my frustration with your lateness reached a boiling point today, and I need to communicate how I've been feeling.

I understand it takes you longer to get ready than it does me. I also know you are able to get out the door on time, when it's really important to you.

When it comes to doing things with me, I feel you aren't as respectful of me or my time. If you think about the last four or five things we've done together, I have had to wait for you for at least 30 minutes.

We were an hour late for dinner at my parent's house and for my client dinner, which was really embarrassing.

When you don't respect my time or my desire to be on time, it feels like you don't care about my feelings. I feel like I have no control over something that's important to me.

Are you willing to make more of an effort to be on time when we go somewhere together? I need to feel you respect me in this way. It's really important to me.

If you are willing, please share with me what you will do to ensure we make it out the door on time for future events. I want to feel secure that us being late doesn't keep happening.

Love,
Jason

Letter #20: No more "silent but deadly" blasts under the sheets.

Dear Jason,

I love you, and that's why I'm having a hard time saying this out loud to you. So here goes . . .

When we are in bed, please try to get up and go to the bathroom if you need to pass gas.

My nose and I would really appreciate it. :)

Love,
Sarah

Section 6
Chores

Letter #21: Being less tidy doesn't mean I don't love you.

Dear Jason,

I love you so much, and I'm really sad when we get into fights like we did yesterday. I'd like to hit the reset button and explain something that I hope will be helpful.

You are right; I have always known that you like a clean and tidy home. In fact, that's something I have always appreciated about you. I'm sure it can be frustrating to like things a certain way in the house and live with someone who doesn't care as much about this.

It is also frustrating for me to feel that my housekeeping standards make you think less of me.

The truth is, I don't care about tidiness as much as you do. Housecleaning feels like a huge drag on my time, when I could be doing something more interesting. Messiness just doesn't push my buttons the way it does for you.

I never mind you asking me to clean something or pick up my stuff. If I don't do it automatically, please don't think it means I don't love or respect you. I feel on the defensive and resistant to cleaning when you get angry or call me a slob. Asking nicely is the best way to invite me to take action.

Here are some ideas to make this easier for both of us. I will clean up the kitchen on nights when you cook dinner, and I will put in 30 minutes a day (15 in the morning and 15 in the evening) to clean or tidy any areas that are bothering you.

I'd like to suggest that we get a housekeeper to come in every other week to do some of the heavy cleaning. If you have other ideas or anything you want to share about this, please write me back.

Love,
Sarah

Letter #22: I feel overwhelmed by work and chores.

Dear Sarah,

We have had quite a week between your big presentation at work and my trip to New York. I'm glad things have calmed down, and we have more time to spend together.

I wanted to share how I'm feeling about all we have going on right now and our division of labor around the house. I feel overwhelmed and stressed, particularly with your request that I clean out the garage and start handling all the bills.

We are both busy, and I know you feel overwhelmed too. I just can't add another thing to my plate right now or in the near future. I think the garage can wait, as it isn't an emergency. Do you agree?

We do need to handle the bills, because they are a priority. Are there any chores you could take off your list, so you could keep handling these for now?

Why don't we write a list of everything we need to do around the house and with household management? Then we can take a good look at what can be postponed (or even delegated to someone else) for now.

Let me know what you think.

Love,
Jason

Letter #23: It feels like you are avoiding your share of chores.

Dear Jason,

I hope you will read this letter in the way I intend it—with love and respect.

There's something that has been on my mind, and I find myself feeling a lot of resentment and frustration. I'm writing so that we can find a solution to this.

Several months ago, you and I sat down and divided the household chores. You agreed to cook and clean up after dinner two nights a week, to clean the bathrooms every Saturday morning, and to wash and fold our clothes every other week.

I agreed to cook and clean three nights a week, tidy the house on Saturday mornings, and to vacuum every other week.

When we discussed this, you said it was a fair division of labor, and you willingly agreed to your set of chores.

In the past few months, you have not done the cooking and cleanup on several of your nights. You have only cleaned the bathroom once this month, and I've been washing my own clothes because you have left them in the hamper.

Barrie Davenport

When I've asked you about this, you have a reason why you can't do your chore, or you say you'll get to it, then you don't. That makes me feel like I have to handle your chores, in addition to my own. I could leave your chores undone. The important thing to me is that we had an agreement.

I feel taken advantage of and disrespected when you passively refuse to follow through, or say you will get the chore done, then don't. My resentment is building, and I hate feeling this way.

I don't want to keep asking you to do your chores, and I know you don't want me nagging you. We can't afford a housekeeper right now, so I'm asking if you will step up and follow through on the chores we agreed on together.

If you want to talk about doing different chores, I'm open to that. I just want it to be an equal division, since we are both working and have such busy lives.

Can you please write back and let me know your thoughts?

Love,
Sarah

Letter #24: Being a woman doesn't mean you can't do "male" chores.

Dear Sarah,

One of the things I most love about you is how strong and accomplished you are. I've always bragged on you about how you can do anything you set your mind to.

That's why I was so surprised this weekend when I asked you to handle mowing the lawn so I could finish my project, and you said no, because it's supposed to be my job as the guy.

We've never really paid much attention to traditional roles in our marriage (I cook and change diapers, and you manage the money!). I don't understand where this is coming from.

Are you uncomfortable using the lawn mower? Do you just not want to do this chore? I know you can do it, if you try, and I really need your help this weekend.

Please let me know what the issue is and how we can work it out.

Love,
Jason

Section 7
Money

Letter #25: I feel anxious and resentful about your debt and spending.

Dear Jason,

This is a hard topic for me to bring up, so I hope you will read this letter in the loving way I intend it.

When we got married, we talked about how important it was to pay down your debt, so we could both start saving toward a down payment on a house.

We agreed that because you make more income, you'd use the difference between your salary and mine to pay down the debt every month.

You haven't been doing that consistently, and we still have a long way to go before it's paid off. I agreed when you wanted to buy a new car last year, even though I didn't feel great about it.

Last month, you bought an expensive new suit, and now you've made arrangements for a weeklong golf trip with your friends. I feel strongly that the $2,000 cost for this trip should go toward the debt and that you need to stop spending money on extras until it's paid off.

I am really anxious about this situation, because I grew up with parents who were always in debt, and I don't want that to happen to us. I'm also resentful because I'm doing my part to save for the house, and you are behind on paying off the debt, while still spending on big-ticket things.

I know it's hard to give up this golf trip, and I understand how much you want to be with your friends. I also know that you and I have a big goal we are working toward.

I need you to prioritize that goal and honor your agreement with me first. I need to feel that I can trust you to be reliable with money and our financial goals. I want to stress how important it is to me that you can meet these needs.

Are you willing to give up the golf trip and apply the money to the debt? Are you willing to stop spending on unnecessary things until it is paid off? Please write me back and let me know.

Love,
Sarah

Letter #26: I feel disrespected when you make financial decisions without me.

Dear Jason,

I love you very much, and I appreciate and respect how hard you are working to provide financially for our family.

I am grateful that I've been able to stay home to raise the kids, which we both agreed was something important to us. We have been a great team this way.

Since we are a team, I'm writing this letter to share something that is really bothering me. When it comes to our finances, I no longer feel like an equal partner with you. This hit home to me again this week, when you made the decision to refinance the house without talking to me first.

I agree with the decision. I don't agree with the way you handled it, by telling me just before I had to sign the paperwork. It made me feel disrespected, like I was an afterthought.

I feel that you view my decision-making power differently when it comes to our finances, ever since I stopped working. You have made several, big, financial decisions without my input during the past year, and I need us to revisit how we will handle these decisions moving forward.

I know I haven't been proactive in asking you questions about our finances, and I also know you haven't stepped forward to include me. Let's start over and work together to make sure we are equal partners in all our financial decisions.

I suggest we sit down twice a month (maybe on the 1st and the 15th) to talk about our spending, saving, and other financial goals. Also, I want to ask you to never make another financial decision without including me early in the process.

Are you agreeable? Please write back and let me know.

Love,
Sarah

Letter #27: I'm feeling frustrated by your spending.

Dear Sarah,

I am so sorry for my part in the argument we had last night. I love you, and I shouldn't have lost my temper and left the room.

I have had time to calm down and think about what is really bothering me.

I know we both make good salaries and can afford to buy things. I wasn't so frustrated with the purchases you made yesterday, as much as I'm frustrated with a pattern of spending without saving enough.

I've been guilty of spending without much thought too, and I know how easy it is to lose track of what has been spent on nonessentials each month.

I looked over our expenses for the past six months, and things are getting out of control. We need to start saving at least $1,000 extra a month to put toward retirement, if we want to live comfortably then.

I would like to review the spreadsheets with you, so you can see exactly where we are and how we can save that money. I suggest we cut back on eating out and shopping for any nonessentials. I am open to any ideas you have about where we can save.

I want us to be in agreement on this, because I don't want to feel like I'm the one driving our financial priorities. I want us to be on the same page.

Please write back and let me know when we can review the spreadsheets.

Love,
Jason

Letter #28: Please stop using guilt trips about spending.

Dear Jason,

I woke up this morning thinking about how much I love you and how much I respect your financial abilities and knowledge. I really appreciate all you do to make sure we stay on track with our financial goals.

Jason, I know you are frugal and that spending on things you don't view as necessary seems wasteful to you. I also know that we are doing fine with our savings and investment goals, and we do have a substantial emergency fund set aside.

I need you to accept and respect that I don't feel as strongly as you do about living so frugally, especially because we are in a good financial position right now. I enjoy eating out a few times a month, and being able to travel is one of my greatest life pleasures. My belief is that as long as we are planning responsibly for the future, we should be able to enjoy ourselves right now.

When you say things to try to make me feel guilty about my expenditures, it is hurtful and frustrating. It takes away the joy I feel in whatever it is I'm doing, and it makes me feel like I'm being controlled. I am not reckless with our money, and that's why these comments are really upsetting.

I am asking that you stop making these negative comments altogether and try harder to understand my point of view. Also, I would like for us to determine a monthly spending budget for nonessential purchases so that we agree upfront. I know we will have different ideas about what this budget should be, and I also think we can find a way to meet in the middle.

I have included my suggestions for this budget below. Please take a look at it, and let me know your thoughts. You are my guy, and I want us to work this out.

Love,
Sarah

Section 8
Affection

Letter #29: It hurts when you hold back affection to get your way.

Dear Sarah,

Do you know how much I love you and how important you are to me? You are the most important person in my life.

This morning, when you asked me to take the trash to the street, I said no, not because I don't care about you or want to help you. I was already running late for my meeting and needed time to review my notes.

You didn't give me time to explain that, and it really hurt when you refused to hug and kiss me goodbye. I felt like you were punishing me, because I didn't comply.

This has happened before, where you won't be affectionate if I don't agree with you, or if I can't do something you ask me to do. My mom did this when I was a kid, if I didn't do what she asked right away. It felt like such a rejection and so manipulative.

115

Sarah, I need to know that you still love and respect me, even when I can't accommodate your requests or agree with you. When you pull away physically, I feel like your affection is conditional, only when I toe the line.

I'm asking that you please stop withholding affection to punish me. I'm happy to talk about any concerns you have about my responses or decisions in a calm and kind way.

Can you honor my request?

Love,
Jason

Letter #30: I need more affection from you.

Dear Jason,

Do you remember when we were first dating, and we spent that rainy weekend at your apartment, cuddled up together on the sofa watching movies?

That is one of my favorite memories, because I loved being so close to you and being held by you.

You may not know how much your affection means to me. When you hug me, hold my hand, and snuggle with me when we are watching TV or in bed, I feel so loved by you.

In the past few years, I feel like you are pulling back from offering me as much physical affection. Now that you have your recliner, we don't sit next to each other at night, and you rarely want to cuddle in bed, even after sex.

I really miss that affection Jason. In fact, I need it to feel connected and close to you. I also need affection to feel sexually desirable.

Is there a reason you are being less affectionate? I hope it's just that we've been together so long, and we have let things slip. If there's more to it, please feel free to share the issue with me, so we can work it out.

Whatever the reason is, I'd like to turn things around and become closer physically again. I'm asking you to be more mindful of offering me affection every day when we are together.

I'd like you to initiate more hugs, kisses, and cuddling together. I'd like you to hold my hand more when we go out. Can you do that?

Please write back and let me know your thoughts.

Love,
Sarah

Letter #31: I'm not comfortable with so much affection in public.

Dear Sarah,

I love you so much, and I'm really sorry I hurt your feelings last night.

I shouldn't have pulled away from you so abruptly when you kissed me at dinner. I know you were being loving and affectionate, which is something I love about you.

I pulled away because my boss and his wife were at the table. I felt uncomfortable kissing in front of them. I promise, I was not rejecting you. I love you and love kissing you. My preference is to show affection in private.

I have never felt comfortable being affectionate in public. My parents never showed public affection, and it just doesn't come easily or naturally for me. I know you were raised differently and feel fine with touching in public, so I'm sure it's hard to understand where I'm coming from.

I'm requesting that you try to respect my feelings about this, even though it's not your preference. If I don't automatically hold your hand or hug and kiss you in front of people, it in no way means I don't desire or love you. I do.

I will try harder to offer more affection around others. We will need to find a compromise on this, because it's not in my comfort zone.

Can you understand my feelings about this? I want to know what you think, so please write back.

Love,
Jason

Letter #32: I feel overwhelmed by your affection.

Dear Jason,

You are the kindest, most loving man. I am grateful you are my husband and so lucky to have you in my life.

I never want to hurt your feelings, and I can tell I wounded you this morning. That wasn't my intention—I don't ever want to hurt you.

I do need to be honest about something that is hard to share, because I fear it might hurt you. I am feeling overwhelmed by the amount of affection and touch you need every day.

I do love you very much, and I like touching you and being touched by you. I just prefer a bit less, especially in the morning when I'm trying to sleep, and you move to my side of the bed to snuggle. I don't have space to move around, and I get really hot and claustrophobic.

I like holding hands on the sofa when we watch TV and cuddling after sex. I like hugging and kissing before we go to work and when we come home. I don't like it when you grab me while I'm cooking, or when I come out of the shower, and I'm trying to get ready for work.

I know you are affectionate because you love me, and I don't want you to stop being that way. I'm just asking that you temper it a little and respect my boundaries about this.

Please let me know how you feel about this and if you can honor my request.

I love you,
Sarah

Section 9
Respect

Letter #33: I feel disrespected when you go to your dad first.

Dear Sarah,

I am writing this letter with love and hope you will read it with a positive mindset. I want our relationship to be strong and respectful.

That's why I'm writing—because in one area, I need to feel more respect from you.

I know how close you and your dad are and what a big support he has been to you all your life. I think your dad is amazing, and I'm grateful to have him as a father-in-law.

Yesterday, when you asked him to come over and fix the dishwasher, because "I wasn't very handy," it really bothered me. I felt that you put your respect for your dad ahead of your concern about me and how I might feel.

I know your dad can easily fix anything around the house. I'm your husband though, and I need you to come to me first. Can you understand that having

121

you and your dad view me as less than capable makes me feel small?

Even though I can't fix everything around the house, I'd prefer that you and I figure out the solution together without calling your dad. We are a team now, and we need to put each other first, even in these small things.

This is really important to me, Sarah. I need to feel that I come first in your eyes. Will you write back and let me know if you can do this?

Love,
Jason

Letter #34: I'm embarrassed when you patronize me in front of friends.

Dear Jason,

You are the most important person in my life, and I hope you know how much I appreciate and love you.

I know you love me too, and that you'd never intentionally hurt me. Last night at dinner, something happened that was hurtful to me, and you may not be aware of it.

Write It Out, Don't Fight It Out

When you were telling our friends about the new house and said that you didn't review the architectural plans with me because you knew I wouldn't understand them, it felt patronizing.

I felt like you viewed me as not intelligent enough to understand the drawings, and it was embarrassing that you shared that opinion with our friends. It made me feel like you don't respect me, both in your opinion about my abilities and your willingness to say this to our friends.

I am an equal partner with you, and even though we may have different strengths, I never question your intelligence or ability to understand something. I am asking the same from you.

I am especially sensitive to being patronized because my dad did it to me all the time growing up and still does sometimes. It's something that makes me feel really diminished.

I need to know that you are proud of me and my abilities and that you won't do this anymore, especially in front of other people. Will you honor that request?

Love,
Sarah

Letter #35: I feel disrespected by your constant reminders.

Dear Sarah,

I'm writing this letter in the hope that we can work through this issue together in a kind and loving way. I know we both feel raw from our fight this morning.

I understand how important it is to you that the guest room is painted before our friends come to stay next week. I want things to look nice for them too.

You asked me to do it last week, and I promised you I would have it done well before they arrive. Since then, you have reminded me about it every day. This morning, I reached my limit when you reminded me again and demanded I do it today. I'm sorry I barked at you—I shouldn't have done that.

I want you to know that I feel disrespected by you when you constantly remind me of something I agreed to do. I feel that you don't trust me to keep my word, or you think I'm not capable of managing my time.

I understand you need time to clean the room after I finish, so I will have the room completed by

Thursday. That is my promise, and I'm asking you to promise you won't remind me again.

In the future, I think a good way to handle any chores you need me to do is to give me a reasonable date when you want the chore completed. If I can meet the deadline or if I need more time, I will let you know right away. Then you need to trust me to handle it without reminding me.

Does that work for you? Please write back and let me know.

Love,
Jason

Letter #36: I feel disrespected when you diminish my role as a mom.

Dear Jason,

I remember so clearly the day that Tyler was born, and you told me how much you loved and respected me for carrying him for nine months and going through a difficult labor to deliver him. I could tell how proud you were of me, and that meant so much.

When we decided that I should stay home to take care of Tyler, and now Amanda, I felt we were on

125

the same page and that you agreed that it was more important for me to be home with the kids than to stay in my job.

I don't know that you see me in the same light anymore. When you make comments about me sitting around the house all day or "just being a taxi driver" to the kids' activities, it feels like you don't value what I do. I'm sure you know I do more than drive the kids and sit around all day.

I know your work is important, and I appreciate and respect all you do to provide for our family. I also know that my work is equally important, because I'm responsible for the two little lives that mean the world to us. I'm also responsible for keeping the house running and in order so that you can more easily manage your job.

When you make comments like you did yesterday, it is so wounding and disrespectful. I am proud of my role as a mom and homemaker, and I want you to be proud too.

I am asking that you not make any more disparaging comments about what I do and that you offer me more words of support and affirmation. We are a team, and we need to respect each other's valuable roles in this family.

Please write back and let me know if you can do this.

Love,
Sarah

Section 10
Emotional Disengagement

Letter #37: I feel disconnected when you are on your phone so much.

Dear Sarah,

You are an amazing woman, and I hope you know how much I love you. From the day we met, I have loved spending time with you. Our time talking and just being together or taking a walk is so important to me.

During the past year or so, there has been one small thing that's come between us and our great talks. It's black and shiny with lots of buttons, and it is getting more and more of your attention. It's your phone. :)

I'm being funny, and I'm also serious. I feel disconnected from you and frustrated by the amount of time you spend looking at stuff on your phone. I really wanted to talk with you at dinner tonight. You were so distracted that we sat there mostly in silence.

I know you aren't intentionally pulling away. Please know that it is hurtful when you would rather look at social media or play an online game than talk with me. I need to believe that you want to spend one-on-one time with me where we are not distracted by other things. I want to know that you value our time together as much as I do.

I'm asking that from now on, you don't bring your phone to the table or to bed at night. Also, when we come home after work, I'd like to spend at least an hour together, where we just talk and reconnect without our phones.

Are you willing to cut back in these ways so we can engage with each other more? I know it will bring us closer, and that's something I think we both want. Please let me know what you think.

Love,
Jason

Letter #38: I feel shut out when you won't tell me what you feel.

Dear Jason,

I am so sorry I stormed out of the room last night. I shouldn't have done that, and I apologize for getting so angry.

I love you so much, and I think that's one of the reasons our conversation was so upsetting to me. When you shut me out and won't talk about what you are feeling, I feel hurt and pushed aside.

I want us to be close and for you to be able to share anything with me. I feel that you don't trust or love me enough to be open and let your feelings show.

I know that your parents never talked about feelings and that it isn't natural for you. This is something that I'm asking you to work on, because it is so important to me.

When you keep your feelings inside, it feels like there's a wall between us. The closeness that we have most of the time is broken, and I feel so alone.

I know it will bring us closer if you open up to me more, and I promise I will always treat your confidences with respect and kindness. Will you try to let me in more, even when it's uncomfortable? I want to stress how important and necessary this is for me.

Please write back and tell me what you think (and feel)!

Love,
Sarah

Letter #39: I am sad we don't spend much time together.

Dear Sarah,

I hope you have a fun trip this weekend with your sister. I will miss you and look forward to Sunday when you come home.

I am happy you and your sister will have this time together. I was bothered, though, when you told me you have another full weekend planned with your friends after you come back.

It seems that during the past year we have spent more time apart than we ever have. Between my work travels, your weekends away, and our various weeknight commitments, we hardly have any time together. It makes me feel sad and disconnected from the woman I fell in love with.

I love you, Sarah, and I want us to do fun things and travel and talk the way we always have. I want us to take weekend trips together and make more plans in advance, so we aren't left wondering what to do on weekends.

Will you please write back and tell me if you've noticed this disconnection, and let me know if anything is bothering you that might be making you pull away? Do you want to spend more time together and work on our closeness?

I do, and I hope you do too.

Love,
Jason

Letter #40: I don't feel safe being honest with you.

Dear Jason,

More than anything in the world, I want our marriage to work and for us to be a happy couple. That's why I'm writing you this letter.

I always want to be the person you can talk to about your feelings or whatever might be bothering you, even if it's something I might not like.

I want you to feel safe sharing things with me, and I'll do my best to love and accept you without criticism, shaming, or judgment.

I need to feel that same acceptance from you, and right now I don't feel safe being honest and open with you.

I was so hurt when you told me I was being selfish and impractical for wanting to change jobs. I was trying to express how unhappy and unfulfilled I feel at work, and you focused only on how it would impact you.

This has happened before—when I try to share something that I feel or that I'm trying to figure out, and you criticize me or diminish me. It happened just last week when I was telling you about how my dad put me down, and you told me to just get over it and stop being so sensitive.

I feel more and more like I have to protect my emotions around you, because I don't feel you will show care and acceptance of me. I am hesitant to share things with you for fear of how you will react, which is putting a wedge between us.

I want us to be close again, and I need to know I have your kindness and support, even if you disagree with what I'm saying. I want you to know that this has become a serious issue for me and something that needs to be addressed.

Are you willing to address it? Please write back to let me know you understand what I'm asking and how I feel about this problem.

Love,
Sarah

Section 11
Sex

Letter #41: I need more variety in our sex life.

Dear Sarah,

You are so beautiful, and I hope you know how attracted I am to you. I love making love with you and how close I feel to you when we do.

I'm writing to let you know that I'd like to explore more with our sex life together. We have gotten into a bit of a rut with the same foreplay and positions every time. We always have sex in our bedroom, and it always starts the same way.

I know you've been uncomfortable with some of the things I've suggested in the past. I'm just asking that we try. I want us both to feel completely comfortable asking for what we want and trying new things. If we try something and you don't enjoy it, I will never pressure you to do it again.

One thing I'd really like would be for you to initiate oral sex more often, and I'd like you to tell me things I can do that would please you. I think it would be fun and exciting for us to come up with new ways to make love, in different places and different positions.

Are you open to that and to initiating oral sex more often? Please write back and let me know, and tell me what you would like to enhance our sex life.

Love,
Jason

Letter #42: I feel a loss of desire with your weight gain.

Dear Jason,

I know you were frustrated last night when I didn't want to make love. I'm sorry I wasn't in the mood and especially sorry that I hurt your feelings. I love you, and I don't want to hurt you.

Write It Out, Don't Fight It Out

That's why it's been so hard for me to be upfront about why I'm not as interested in sex as I used to be. This is difficult to express, and I want to begin by letting you know that I believe it is a fixable issue.

When we first married, you were in such great shape, working out several times a week. You motivated me to exercise more to keep up with you.

During the past several years, your weight gain has worried me for your health, and it's also impacted my desire for sex. You and I have always had a great physical connection, and I want us to have that again. To me, a fit, healthy man is really sexy.

I know you feel bad about your weight, and I don't want to add to your pain about it. I do know that you can lose the weight to get back in shape, and that you will be happier and healthier if you do.

Jason, I will always love you, no matter what. I would very much like you to lose weight so we can enjoy the same amazing sex life we used to have.

Are you willing to start working on it? I will work with you, and we can exercise together. Please write back and let me know what you think.

Love,
Sarah

Letter #43: I feel neglected when you are too exhausted for sex.

Dear Sarah,

Thank you so much for all you do to take care of our family and raise the kids. You are amazing, and I love you so much.

I know how exhausting it is to manage the kids all day and handle all your chores in the evening. I am trying to pick up more of the slack when I get home from work, so you have a little more down time.

Sarah, I'm feeling neglected and frustrated that our sex life has gotten so sparse, and that you are frequently too tired to have sex. I know we are both worn out at the end of the day. I also know that having regular sex is important for our closeness and connection as a couple.

We need to prioritize this more, because our marriage is the most important part of our lives as a family. I'm sure we can find time to have sex at least once a week.

I have a few ideas for how we can do this. We could ask a babysitter to take the kids out for dinner and an outing once a week in the evening. Or we could try having sex on Saturday mornings, and lock the door while the kids watch cartoons. I'm open to any other suggestions you might have.

Mainly, I want you to know how important it is to me that we get our sex life back on track and work together to make it happen.

Are you onboard? Please write back and let me know your thoughts and any ideas you have.

I love you,
Jason

Letter #44: I feel disrespected when you constantly pressure me for sex.

Dear Jason,

Our fight last night made me realize two things. First, I really love you and want our marriage to work. Second, I don't want to keep fighting about sex. I know you don't either.

The truth is, you and I have different sex drives. As you've said, you'd like sex every day. I'd prefer a few times a month, or once a week at most. It's not because I don't love or desire you. I do desire you, when it doesn't feel obligatory.

Barrie Davenport

When you pressure me for sex or try to make me feel guilty when I say no, I feel disrespected and unappreciated, which throws cold water on my desire.

What makes me want sex more is when you are affectionate, supportive, and loving, without tying it to a sexual outcome. I also need to feel that you respect my differing sexual needs.

I'd like to suggest two things. I would like you to stop asking for sex every day and instead offer me a long hug and some kind words. Also, I suggest we start by agreeing to sex once a week. Weekends are usually best, and we can mix it up. I promise to initiate sex, so you know you don't have to ask.

Are you agreeable to trying this for a couple of months to see how it goes? Please let me know what you think.

Love,
Sarah

Section 12
Jealousy

Letter #45: I feel jealous of your relationship with your boss.

Dear Sarah,

You did an amazing job of arranging your company party. I am so proud of you and how skilled you are. You're going to run that company one day!

I could see how proud your boss was too, and how much he values you as an employee. I have to admit that seeing how well the two of you interact has made me feel a little jealous.

You may not be aware of this, so I wanted to share what I observed. When you are talking with him, you show a level of interest and enthusiasm that I don't see as often at home with me. I know you need to be attentive and extra charming around him, because he's your boss. It's made me realize how much I'd like to be the recipient of that same kind of attention and interest.

Also, for my own peace of mind, I would prefer you maintain a more professional distance from him.

You are a beautiful woman, and I don't want him to have any reason to step over the line.

I don't want to come across as the controlling, jealous husband. I just want you to know what's on my mind and ask you to be more thoughtful of my feelings in your interactions with him and with me.

Do you understand where I'm coming from here? Please write back and let me know what you think.

I love you,
Jason

Letter #46: Your jealousy makes me feel you don't trust me.

Dear Jason,

I'm still reeling from our argument, and I want to work this out because I love you. Let's find a resolution to this issue.

First, I will say without hesitation that you have no reason to mistrust me. I haven't said or done anything with anyone that betrays my vows to you. I hope you believe that.

When you act jealous every time another man speaks to me or smiles at me, it makes me feel like you don't trust me. You act like I don't know how to handle myself appropriately around other men.

I feel embarrassed by your behavior when you intercede and act possessive of me in front of other people when this happens.

I need the freedom to have casual conversations with our male friends and my coworkers without fearing that you will get upset and make a scene. I am not flirting or inviting attention. Your jealousy is putting a wedge between us and causing problems that shouldn't exist, because there is no foundation for them.

I really want us to have a strong and happy marriage, so I need you to stop with the jealous behaviors and accusations and work on trying to figure out where these feelings are coming from and why you don't trust me. This is not sustainable for me, and I hope you will honor my request.

I am open to hearing your thoughts and feelings about this, so please write back.

Love,
Sarah

Letter #47: Your jealousy of our neighbors is taking a toll on us.

Dear Sarah,

When we got married, I knew I had everything I wanted and needed with you and now our children. I am content with our life together, even though we aren't wealthy and live modestly.

I just wish you felt that same level of contentment. It has become obvious to me that you feel envious of the Thompsons, with Jack's promotion and their new house.

When you make comments about how much money they have and what they can do that we can't, it makes me feel like you don't appreciate what you have with me and our family. I may not make as much money; however, I hope you agree that we live a good life and have many blessings.

Sarah, you have a husband who loves you dearly, two beautiful children, a comfortable home, a secure job, and many wonderful friends. I am asking that you try to be more content with the life we have.

Please stop focusing on the Thompsons so much and talking about your frustrations related to them.

It is adding pressure to me and to our relationship that doesn't need to be there. I am happy in my career. I doubt that it will ever afford me the income level that Jack has.

Can you accept that and work on being less jealous of the Thompsons? I want you to be happy, Sarah, and I hope you can find happiness in the life we have.

Love,
Jason

Letter #48: I feel hurt by your flirtatiousness when we go out.

Dear Jason,

Thank you for planning our dinner and dancing outing last night with Bill and Julia. You are great at coming up with fun things to do and making sure everyone is enjoying themselves. I really love that about you—among other things!

As much fun as I had, something has been bothering me all day, and I need to share it with you. After you had a few drinks last night, you started flirting a lot with Julia and with that girl at the bar.

I know you weren't trying to hurt me and that you were just having fun. I did feel hurt though, because it was disrespectful to me as your wife. It feels insensitive and embarrassing, especially since Julia saw what you were doing.

Please take a moment and think about how you would feel if I flirted with Bill or some other attractive guy. You would probably feel jealous and upset, just as I felt when it was happening to me.

We are a committed couple, and I need to feel safe that you won't be offering your romantic attention to another woman, no matter how innocent it seems to you.

This is a big deal to me, and I'm asking you to honor my request and stop flirting with other people. Are you willing to do that? Please let me know.

Love,
Sarah

Section 13
Kids

Letter #49: I feel disrespected when you undermine my parenting rules.

Dear Sarah,

I wanted to finish the discussion we started last night before the kids came into the room. First, I want you to know that I think you are an amazing, caring mom to our children. I respect and love all that you do for them.

The problem I had last night was when you told Stephanie she could spend the night out, when I had already told her she couldn't. It felt disrespectful to have you contradict a rule I had already implemented, and I feel it sends the wrong message to the children when we aren't on the same page in front of them.

I know you think Stephanie needs to be more social, and that's why you wanted her to go to the sleepover. I also know that we have a rule about no sleepovers on a weekend preceding a big test at school—which Stephanie has on Wednesday. That's why I said no.

When you undermine my parenting rules by changing them without first talking with me, I feel you are violating a trust we have together. We need to be a united team in front of the kids, and if we disagree about parenting, we should work it out privately and reach a solution together.

I'm asking that going forward you don't override a rule that I have implemented, and I won't do that to you. Also, I would like to have another joint discussion with Stephanie and tell her that we have both decided she can go to her friend's house and stay until 10:00 pm, but she can't sleep over.

Are you onboard with both these requests? Please write back and let me know.

Love,
Jason

Letter #50: I need for you to step up more with the kids.

Dear Jason,

I'm sorry I got so irritated with you this morning. I shouldn't have slammed the door when I left the room, and I apologize for that. I do love you very much.

Write It Out, Don't Fight It Out

Here's the deal. I am feeling increasingly frustrated and upset about our division of labor with the kids. I need an equal parenting partner with you, both in disciplining and taking care of them. We both work full-time jobs, yet I am doing the majority of the childcare and discipline.

This morning, I was busy preparing breakfast and making lunches while the kids were having a meltdown about getting dressed. Instead of managing the problem and making sure they were ready on time, you went in your office and closed the door, leaving me to handle everything.

Jason, this happens in some way almost every day, and it is affecting my relationship with you. I am feeling more and more resentful and hurt that you aren't stepping up to handle your share of this important job in our family. Also, the kids need to see that both parents are involved in setting and enforcing rules—not just Mom.

I need you to make sure the kids are dressed and ready on time for school in the mornings, while I get their food and backpacks ready. Also, in the evenings, when they misbehave or break a rule, I'd like you to more often discuss and implement consequences. We can continue to take turns preparing dinner and getting the kids to bed.

Jason, will you agree to be a more equal parenting partner and step up in the ways I've requested? Please write back and let me know.

Love,
Sarah

Letter #51: I need you to let me parent in my own way.

Dear Sarah,

I love you very much, and I am so grateful you are willing to be home with the kids while they are young. You are a fantastic mom.

It is true that you spend more time with the kids than I do and that you've read more parenting books. I respect all that you know about raising our children the right way. I want you to offer that same respect to me.

When I'm with the kids, and you jump in and tell me what to do, I feel like you don't trust my judgment and ability to be a good parent. It hurts when you suggest you know more because I'm not home all day.

Though we may not always do things the same way, I think those little differences can be good for our children. They see there is more than one way to respond and that we can differ and still be good parents.

We are on the same page about most of the big things, such as house rules and consequences. I'm asking that you let go of the little differences and allow me to be myself as a dad without judgment or jumping in to take over.

If you feel strongly about something, I will always listen and take it to heart. If we disagree, we can work to reach a compromise. Most of all, I want you to show more respect and trust in me as a parent.

Can you do that? Please write back and let me know.

Love,
Jason

Letter #52: I feel ignored when you focus so much time on the kids.

Dear Jason,

Thank you for being such a hands-on, loving father to our children. They are so fortunate to have you as their dad, and I love you even more for being such a wonderful parent.

Before we had children, we talked about how our marriage should always come first and that you and I should be the center of our family. I know we both believe that a strong marriage is necessary for raising secure and happy kids.

Lately, I've been feeling that the focus has shifted for you, and that your priority is more the children than it is me and our relationship. I am glad that you are such an involved parent. I need you to be as involved with me and the health of our marriage.

When we get home from work, rather than allowing the kids to interrupt us and monopolize the conversation, I would like for us to have time to ourselves to catch up and reconnect without them.

I want the kids to see that you put our special time together first, ahead of their demands or even your desire to play with them right away.

Also, I'd like to ask that you not fall asleep in Tyler's room when you put him to bed, and instead shorten the bedtime routine and come back to our room, so we have more time together alone in the evening.

Finally, I'd like for us to commit to getting away for a weekend, just the two of us, once a quarter, so we have some extended time together without the kids. My parents are always willing to watch them for us.

I love our children as much as you do, and I know that it will only benefit them to see how committed their parents are to each other. Do you agree? Are you willing to honor my requests? Please write back and let me know.

Love,
Sarah

Section 14
Career

Letter #53: I'm frustrated that you bring your work home.

Dear Sarah,

I love you, and I'm so proud of all that you've accomplished in your career. You are such a dedicated employee, and I hope your boss knows how fortunate he is to have you!

As your responsibilities have grown at work, I've noticed during the past year that you are bringing work home more and more often. I understand the pressure you feel to do a good job. I also see that

151

the time you spend working at night and on the weekends is affecting our relationship.

When you are so distracted and busy with work when we are home together, I feel lonely and disconnected from you. I miss our long talks in the evenings and the freedom we had to travel on the weekends.

I know your job is important to you, and I think our marriage is even more important to both of us. I don't want your work to put a wedge between us and erode the closeness we've always had.

Do you agree with this? If so, what can you do to back off this pattern and leave your work at the office? Please write back and let me know your thoughts.

Love,
Jason

Letter #54: I feel you think your career is more important than mine.

Dear Jason,

I am so proud of you for getting offered this job in Chicago. You are so talented, and I can understand why the company wants you there so badly.

Write It Out, Don't Fight It Out

I didn't mean for your announcement about this to turn into an argument, and I'm sorry I reacted negatively as soon as you said something. I understand why that upset you. I want to share my perspective in a calmer way in this letter.

Jason, when we moved here for your job five years ago, I agreed to it, even though I loved my job in Boston. I made a sacrifice so that you could have this opportunity and pursue your career goals.

Now I've started my own consultancy here in Denver, and I've built a great client base. I feel resentful and frustrated that you are asking me to pull up roots again and start over with my business that I've worked so hard to grow.

I feel that you don't value my career happiness and goals as much as you do your own, and that you think your career path should always come first.

I understand that this new job in Chicago will have a higher salary. For me, the money isn't the primary consideration. I love what I do, and I love the people I work with. My business is getting traction, and I'm excited about that.

Yes, you make more money than I do, and we both enjoy the benefits of your salary. I don't think that fact should trump all the other considerations that are in play here. I love my work and our life in Denver. I don't want to leave.

I'm asking that you make the sacrifice this time and turn down the offer. I know it will be hard for you, and I understand how disappointed you will feel. I also know that many more opportunities in Denver will come your way, and that we have a great life here together.

More than anything, your willingness to pass up this offer will show me that you see me as an equal partner, and you are willing to put my career goals first this time. That will mean the world to me.

Please think this over for a while, and write back with your thoughts.

I love you,
Sarah

Letter #55: I'm uncomfortable that you make more money.

Dear Sarah,

I really blew it this morning. I'm so sorry I made that stupid comment about you wearing the pants in the family. I love you, and I'm so proud of all that you've achieved in your career.

Write It Out, Don't Fight It Out

I think my thoughtless comment gave you a small window into my heart. As proud as I am of you, I admit I feel uncomfortable that you make more money than I do.

It sometimes makes me insecure that you and other people might think I don't measure up or that I'm leeching off you.

I know this is old-school thinking. I just want to be open with you, so you know why I sometimes react the way I do. I'm not making an excuse for my comment. I'm just letting you know that I struggle with it from time to time.

I want you to feel proud of me, and yes, there's a part of me that wants to be the main provider, because that's how it was in my family and society reinforces that.

As I write this letter, I think what I need from you is the reassurance that you aren't resentful of me or think less of me because of our salary disparity.

Please let me know what you think.

Love,
Jason

Letter #56: I want to go back to work.

Dear Jason,

We've had a hard time talking about this subject in the past, so I'm writing today in the hope that we can work this out without anger. I love you, and I don't want this issue to put a distance between us.

I know we agreed before the kids were born that I would be their primary caretaker and quit my full-time job. I also understand how demanding your job is and how much time it requires.

What I didn't anticipate is how much I would miss my job and how much I need to work to feel fulfilled. I love our children, and I'm so glad I've been able to spend these years with them at home. Now I am past ready to go back to a full-time job, and we need to figure something out to make that work for all of us.

Yes, it will likely mean that you'll have to step in more. I know that seems overwhelming to you with the demands of your job. I also know you do have some flexibility with your work schedule.

We are partners in our family and co-parents to our children, and I feel it is time there's more balance in our roles. I'm sure that between us we can figure out a way to make this work, even if we need to hire a sitter to help out.

I need you to stop saying it's impossible for me to go back to work, and instead adopt a more positive attitude and help me create a workable plan. I suggest we sit down and go through the kids' schedules and activities and decide how we can divide and conquer—or find someone to help us, if necessary.

This is important to me Jason, and I need to know I have your full support both in word and action. Can you do that? Please let me know.

Love,
Sarah

Section 15
In-Laws

Letter #57: I feel you don't support me when your parents are rude.

Dear Sarah,

I love you, and I see our relationship as my top priority over anyone else in my life. You and the kids are my family, and nothing is more important than the three of you. I need to know that you feel the same about me as your husband.

I know how much it pains you when your parents and I don't get along. I understand how hard it is to stand up to them. You must know that their rude and unkind comments are hurtful to me. What's more hurtful, though, is that you try to appease them, when I respond to their remarks, rather than support me.

When you don't speak up and set a clear boundary by saying their behavior is unacceptable, it gives them permission to keep making digs at my expense. It seems you are prioritizing their feelings over mine, and this is not the way a healthy marriage should be.

The situation this weekend with your parents was the last straw for me. I need you to step up, and let your parents know that I am your first priority, and that you'll no longer tolerate their rude behavior toward me.

I am asking that you call them today, and let them know that we will leave the house (or they will have to leave ours) the next time they make a sarcastic or cutting remark about me. As their daughter, you need to step up and do this, rather than asking me to do it.

I want to have a good relationship with your parents, and I will always welcome them in our lives, if they treat me and our family with kindness and respect. It may take some time for them to learn that you and I are serious about how they can and can't treat me.

Are you willing to make the call and set these boundaries with them? Will you put my feelings and our marriage first, ahead of your parents?

Please write back and let me know.

Love,
Jason

Letter #58: Your mom is interfering with our childrearing too much.

Dear Jason,

I am so sorry I made that snide remark about your mom last night. It was inappropriate, and I shouldn't have said it. I love your mom, and she has been a huge help to us. She is generous in helping with the kids, and I really appreciate that.

I'm having trouble figuring out how to balance her generosity with all the comments and suggestions she makes about how we are raising them.

I know it's easier for you to brush her comments aside, because you are her son. When she criticizes me, or tells me how I should be doing things differently, I feel stung and resentful. Also, it's frustrating when she ignores or overrides rules we've set for the kids. I don't think it's her place to do this or to offer criticism or advice, unless we ask for it.

You and I have made our own decisions about how we want to raise our children, and we shouldn't have to defend them. I want your mom to have a good relationship with the kids and with me. That's hard when she interferes with our parenting or undermines our rules.

I want things to be comfortable and happy for all of us when we're together. I'm asking that you speak with your mom about the situation before we see her again to ask her to back off with the criticism and advice and abide by our rules for the children.

Will you do that? Please write back and let me know your thoughts.

Love,
Sarah

Letter #59: I don't want to spend the holidays with your parents.

Dear Sarah,

This is a hard letter to write, so please read it knowing how much I love you and want you to be happy.

When your parents called today about their plans for us to spend the week at their house for the Christmas holidays, I found myself feeling resentful and frustrated.

I know this has been a tradition in your family for years, and I could see how excited you were on the phone with them. I love your parents, and we've had many great times there.

We've gone to your parents' house every Christmas since we've been married, and it's become an automatic assumption that we do this each year. I really want to do something different this year. I also don't want your parents to keep assuming we'll spend every holiday with them.

We haven't been able to establish our own family traditions around Christmas, and I want us to do that. I'd like to spend the week before Christmas and Christmas Day at our house with the kids.

Then maybe we can go on a road trip the week after and visit your parents for a day or two on the way. We can create some fantastic traditions and memories for our children and have more flexibility to go to some of the holiday parties and events here that we usually miss.

Sarah, I know this is hard for you, and I understand. Please, remember I have gone along with your wishes on this for many years. Now I'm asking that you respect my wishes going forward. Will you please let your parents know that we have made different plans this year, and that in the future we won't always be available to spend the holidays with them?

Please let me know what you think.

Love,
Jason

Letter #60: Your parents need to stop pressuring us to have kids.

Dear Jason,

It was a great weekend with your mom and dad. Thank you for arranging everything and planning the family dinner. You are amazing, and I love you.

Write It Out, Don't Fight It Out

Something came up this weekend, again, that has really been bothering me, and I need to share it with you. Every time we are with your parents, they say something to me about having kids. They make it sound as though I'm being selfish and weird for not wanting to get pregnant right now.

Your mom mentioned this time that she's the only person in her book club who doesn't have grandchildren, and your dad reminded me that I'm getting so old I might have trouble getting pregnant if I don't get on it.

I know they want grandchildren and are eager for us to get started. Their comments are beginning to feel pushy and invasive. I feel on edge around them, because I know they will bring it up.

Will you please talk to your parents about this, and let them know that you and I are on the same page about waiting to have children? Will you ask them to stop asking us about it or making comments about it?

I know neither of us want this issue to make it uncomfortable to be around your mom and dad. Please write back and tell me what you think.

Love,
Sarah

Section 16
Friends

Letter #61: I feel your friends are an unhealthy influence on our marriage.

Dear Sarah,

I'm so glad you had a fun weekend with your girlfriends. I know it was relaxing to get away and spend some time at the beach.

I'm having difficulty with something related to your weekend away that I need to share with you. I saw your friend's Facebook pictures during the weekend, and I was really upset by many of them.

It was clear that you were drunk in the photos, and in several of the pictures you were dancing with other guys. I never see you behave this way, except when you are with this group of women. It is embarrassing and hurtful to me, and I don't want it to happen again.

Everyone in the group is single except you, and I know you want to join in the fun when you are with them. The fun they are having isn't appropriate for a married woman—especially because our kids and friends have access to Facebook and can see the photos.

Sarah, something like this happened the last time you got together with this group of friends. I know they encourage you to cut loose, and they don't seem to realize how it might impact my relationship with you. I need it to stop, and I'm asking that you no longer go on weekend getaways like this with them. Will you honor this?

Also, I'm wondering the deeper reason behind your choice of these friends and your behavior? Why would you behave this way knowing that it would be hurtful to me?

Please write back and help me understand this.

Love,
Jason

Letter #62: I'm hurt when you spend so much time with your friends.

Dear Jason,

Thank you for making me breakfast in bed this morning. I know you were trying to make up for last night, and I appreciate the gesture.

We were both angry last night and didn't really reach a resolution, so I wanted to write to let you know what I'm feeling.

I am glad that you have a great group of friends to spend time with, and I really like the guys you hang out with. What is bothering me isn't that you have friends. It's how much time you spend with them.

Between your softball league, Wednesday poker night, and the nights you go out for beers after work, you and I spend only a few hours together a week. It makes me feel like I'm a lower priority to you than your friends are.

I would like for us to spend more time doing things together as a couple on the weekends. I'd also like you come home straight after work on nights when you don't have poker, so that we can spend time talking and eat dinner together.

Are you committed to growing our relationship, Jason? If so, you will need to invest more time in it by spending more time with me. Will you write back and let me know what you are willing to do to cut back on time with the guys and spend more time with me?

Love,
Sarah

Letter #63: You need to develop some outside friendships.

Dear Sarah,

I am so sorry you've had such a difficult few days. I love you so much and hate to see you suffering.

I wish I could have responded the way you needed me to when you told me about the fight with your mom. I may be too close to the situation, because it has gone on for a while, and we've talked about it a lot.

I want to be a support for you, Sarah. I just don't think I can always offer you the kind of perspective you might need in situations like this. I'm also feeling a little overwhelmed by how much you need to talk about this issue. I don't know what else I can say, and I know that's hurting your feelings.

I think it would be a big help for both of us if you developed more female friends who can be an additional support system for you. As much as I want to be everything for you, I think having other people in your life who you can talk to would be a positive step.

You've always said that I'm the only person you need. I'm flattered that you feel that way. I just think it is healthier for both of us if you broaden your circle and develop more friendships.

I want to hear your thoughts on this.

Love,
Jason

Letter #64: I'm not comfortable with your opposite-sex friend.

Dear Jason,

I've thought about whether or not I should write this letter several times. I think it is better for our relationship that I share this with you. I love you, and I don't want anything to come between us.

I know you and Ellen have been friends for years, and you've assured me it is strictly platonic on your part. I sense that it's more than that for Ellen.

She says and does things that make me feel she has a romantic interest in you, and it is making me deeply uncomfortable. There is a coziness she has with you that is inappropriate for just a friend. On several occasions, she's acted competitive with me by saying she thinks she knows you better than I do and that the two of you have a "special connection." Can you see how that makes me feel?

Jason, I know you don't want me to feel threatened or uncomfortable with your friendship with Ellen. The truth is, I do, and I don't like feeling that way. I don't like wondering or questioning what's going on when you spend time with her or she texts you.

I am fine if we do things in groups with Ellen and your other friends. I'm no longer okay with you spending time with her alone. I am asking that you stop socializing with just her and that you ask her to stop texting you to chat. If she needs to reach us, she can send a message to our joint email address.

I would like you to clarify with her the new boundaries of your relationship and why you need to be respectful of me as your wife by doing this (without casting the blame on me).

Are you willing to honor my requests? Please let me know.

Love,
Sarah

Section 17
Reliability

Letter #65: I feel disrespected when you don't follow through on your promises.

Dear Sarah,

Thank you for reading this letter. Please know I write it with love, and I hope you read it with an open mind and heart.

I admit I was really let down this morning when you showed up late for my presentation at church. I worked so hard on it, and I wanted to see your smiling, supportive face on the front row. You promised me yesterday you would be there on time, and I felt so deflated to see you come in 20 minutes late.

Sarah, you have a habit of not following through on your promises to me and then making excuses about why you didn't follow through. Last week, you said you would handle the bills by the end of the weekend, and they are still sitting on your desk. You frequently promise to work with me in the yard, only to back out once I get started, like you did last time.

The main point for me is feeling that I can't rely on you to keep your word. Now, when you tell me you'll do something, I find myself wondering if it will really happen. It is further hurtful when you offer a weak excuse.

I would much rather you say you can't or won't do something upfront, than tell me you will and then not follow through. I don't like mistrusting your word or the disappointed feeling I get when you try to justify a broken promise.

A relationship has to be built on trust, Sarah, even in the small things. I need to know I can count on you with the small things, so that I have trust in you when the big things occur.

I'm asking that you be more mindful of what you agree to do, and that when you do agree, you follow through as you promised. If something truly unforeseen happens, of course, that is an exception, Lately, this has become more the rule than the exception.

Are you willing to try harder with this? I want to rely on you, Sarah, and know that your word is gold. Let me know what you think.

Love,
Jason

Letter #66: I never know how you will react.

Dear Jason,

I am so sorry you had such a bad day at work yesterday. I can only imagine how disappointing it was to lose that client. I always want to be a support to you when things like this happen.

I was really thrown for a loop when you yelled at me and told me I was lazy for not having dinner ready. I understand you were in a funk about the client. I can't understand your aggressive and unkind reaction to me. It was hurtful and unnecessary, especially when I was trying to be supportive.

Jason, you may not be aware of your inconsistent reactions and behaviors with me. You can be so loving and attentive at times, and then out of the blue, you either get really angry or you pull away completely. I never know how you will react to things, and it makes me feel like I'm walking on eggshells.

When we first met, I could always count on your steadiness and loving words. Now, I feel less and less like I know how you'll react to me. Will I get the loving Jason or the guy who is edgy and angry?

This isn't sustainable, as it's causing me a lot of anxiety. I know we all have bad days. This seems to be more than that for you. I need to know I can count on your love, kindness, and support most of the time.

If stress is contributing to this behavior, then you need to find a way to manage the stress so you don't take it out on me. Are you willing to figure out how to be more consistently kind and calm with me? What can you do to work this out?

Please write back and let me know.

Love,
Sarah

Letter #67: When you overpromise to others, it impacts me.

Dear Sarah,

I am always amazed at how much you accomplish and how generous you are with other people. I love that about you.

I was surprised today when you told me you agreed to be the chair of the PTA. That's a huge job that will last all year, and I wish you had discussed it with me before accepting the position.

Between your job, your volunteer work at the hospital, and your agreement to help on the neighborhood association, I don't know how much more we can fit into our lives. I say "we" because your promises to other people also impact me and the kids.

It prevents us from spending time together as a family, and I have to pick up the slack at home with the kids' activities and chores. I need to rely on you to put our family's needs first and to be willing to say no to outside requests. I need to know I can count on you to handle your share of our family obligations.

Is there any way to turn down the PTA position? If not, would you be willing to drop one of your other commitments? Also, going forward I'm asking that you not commit to anything else without first talking to me. Will you honor this request?

Please write back and tell me your thoughts.

Love,
Jason

Write It Out, Don't Fight It Out

Letter #68: I feel you aren't there for me when I need you.

Dear Jason,

I am still hurt and angry, but I do want you to know I love you. I hate it when we fight, and I'm writing in hopes you will really hear what I'm trying to say.

I need you to understand my feelings about this weekend. My surgery was just a week ago, and even though I'm doing better, I still need help. I get so tired during the day and exhausted in the evening. After dealing with all the chores and childcare, the end of the day is overwhelming.

I know you want to go on this golf weekend with your friends. I just can't manage on my own without you here, and I'm hurt that you are still pressing to go. I wish you would have said no to the trip without me having to ask you to.

I feel that when I am sick or incapacitated in some way, you get frustrated rather than more attentive and helpful. You aren't there for me when I need you the most.

I'm not sure why my times of weakness make you less available to me. Can you help me understand that? I need to rely on the person I love most to take care of me and support me when I'm down or sick. I want to do that for you.

I need your help this weekend, Jason, and I'm asking you to please stay home and allow me to recover more from the surgery. Can you do that with love and without resentment?

Love,
Sarah

Section 18
Infidelity

Letter #69: I have a suspicion you are cheating on me.

Dear Sarah,

This is a hard letter to write, because I am afraid of the answer. I love you, and despite what you might tell me, I want your honesty.

I suspect that you are having an affair.

Your behavior has been different during the past few months, and I couldn't put my finger on it. Then I noticed how you no longer let me pick up your cellphone when it buzzes. Also, you haven't wanted to make love for a long time and always have a reason why we can't.

Last night, you were supposed to be at Lee Ann's house. When I called there, she said you never had plans to be there. You lied to me about it when you got home.

It all added up last night after I called Lee Ann, and it seems the signs are clear. I hope I'm wrong. I need you to be honest with me. Are you seeing someone else? Are you in love with someone else?

I feel sick right now with fear and pain. I need to hear the truth from you. I don't know that I can talk face to face now, so please write me back.

Love,
Jason

Letter #70: I still feel hurt and angry about your affair.

Dear Jason,

I love you, and I do want to commit to our marriage again. I need you to understand that I'm still having a hard time.

Barrie Davenport

As much as I want to forgive you, and I do forgive you on one level, I'm still so devastated by your affair. Some days I feel blindsided by the betrayal of my trust and our marriage vows. I still have images in my head of you and Sharon together, and it makes me physically ill.

I know you are ready for us to move past this, and I believe you when you say you are fully committed to me and have no feelings for Sharon. I do want things to work between us. My emotions still have to catch up. The wound is raw, even though it's been a year, and sometimes I feel so angry and hurt I could scream.

I am asking you to be more patient with my healing process and the rebuilding of my trust in you. The more transparent you are with me about where you have been and what you are doing, the more I feel safe with you. When you hug me, let me cry, and let me feel angry, the more I believe you will stick by me.

I can't give you a date when I will feel completely healed and trusting again. You will have to ride this out with me, just as I rode it out with you when this all happened.

I need you to allow me to go through this process without pressure or visible frustration with my emotions. Can you do that?

Love,
Sarah

Letter #71: I need you to forgive me and stop punishing me for cheating.

Dear Sarah,

I want to reiterate in writing how much I love you and how committed I am to our marriage. If I could go back in time and erase my behavior, you know I would.

I am so sorry for the tremendous pain my affair caused you and equally sorry for the erosion of trust my actions have caused. I hope that I continue to show you in word and deed that I am faithful to you and honest with you.

Sarah, I am writing today to ask you to please fully forgive me for the affair. It has been more than three years now, and I have gone through counseling and worked hard to be a better man.

I want our marriage to be happy and strong, and I will continue to be as transparent with you as you

179

need to feel safe with me. I am asking that you stop bringing up the affair in our disagreements or using it to wound me.

If you have accepted my apologies, agree that I have proven my faithfulness in these three years, and still want us to be married, I hope you can take the step to fully forgive me.

Are you able to do that, Sarah? Can we move on in our marriage and find happiness and mutual trust again?

Please write back and let me know your thoughts.

Love,
Jason

Letter #72: I have feelings for someone else and I'm concerned.

Dear Jason,

This is a hard letter to write, and I hope it will be the beginning of a dialogue between us that is kind and respectful.

I have debated about whether or not to say anything, especially given my own confusion. I've decided to go ahead, because you are my husband and deserve honesty.

Jason, I have feelings for someone else. We are not having a physical affair. I am attracted to him and he to me. This is someone from my work you don't know. I have known him for about six weeks.

I've been feeling guilty about this situation and wanted to tell you earlier. Honestly, I've been caught by surprise by my feelings and the best way to deal with them.

I have gone to see a counselor to talk about everything and what to do next. I'm sure you will want to know if I love this man and if I intend to end our marriage. The answer is I don't know right now. I'm too confused.

You and I have many issues we haven't resolved, and in light of what I'm sharing with you, my feelings about our marriage are unsettled. I think the best course of action now is for us to go to marriage counseling and put everything out there to see where we stand.

I did not intend for this to happen Jason, and I feel awful about hurting you with this information. Are you willing to go to see a counselor with me? That is where I would like to talk through everything with you so we have someone to help us navigate this.

Please write back and let me know.

Love,
Sarah

Section 19
Politics and Religion

Letter #73: I feel shut down by your political opinions.

Dear Sarah,

I'm sorry we had such a heated argument last night. I love you, and I can't stand it when we fight. I'd like for us to start over fresh today.

I've always been proud of what a strong and principled woman you are. I understand how much this political season has frustrated and upset you, and I totally respect your feelings and opinions. We are on the same page most of the time.

What is difficult for me is when you shut down my opinions, if they don't exactly match yours. When I started to share my thoughts last night about the election, you got angry and kept interrupting me to tell me I was wrong.

It feels like we can't have a calm and civil conversation about this topic, especially if I don't agree with everything you say. I do have valid points. It often feels like you don't hear them.

I am asking that you give my opinions the same respect I give yours, and that you listen more to me and try to understand what I'm saying without anger or a quick rebuttal.

Will you honor my request about this, Sarah? I would like us to be able to talk about anything together without either of us walking on eggshells.

Please write back and tell me your thoughts.

Love,
Jason

Letter #74: Let's agree not to talk about politics.

Dear Jason,

I am proud of the way we've been able to handle our political differences throughout the years and not allow them to come between us. I love that we've been able to talk and joke about it and not get upset with each other.

This political season has felt different. We both have such strong feelings about our positions that it's seeping into our relationship. As much as I'd like to have open and civil discussions, I find myself feeling frustrated and angry that we aren't on the same page. You may be feeling the same way.

I don't want our political differences to infect our closeness and love for each other. There is too much good about our relationship to allow politics to cause problems for us.

I am asking that we agree not to discuss politics or allow ourselves to be pulled into political conversations with friends and family. It is a slippery slope than seems to end unhappily too many times.

Let's try to protect our marriage by steering clear of a topic we know will only cause division between us.

Are you in agreement with this? Please write back and let me know your thoughts.

Love,
Sarah

Letter #75: Please stop trying to convert me.

Dear Sarah,

I'm sorry I walked out of the room last night. I shouldn't have shut you down, and I apologize for doing that.

When we first started dating, I was upfront about my religious views. I told you why I left the church, and that I couldn't see myself ever accepting those beliefs again. You seemed to be fine with that at the time, and I was fine with how strongly you feel about your faith.

You have been subtly pressuring me with comments about why I need to change my position, and you leave books out for me to read to try to convert me. Last night, when you brought it up again, it felt like you never really heard me when I first shared my feelings on this. Maybe you heard and thought you could change me.

Sarah, I respect your faith and totally support your desire to go to church and participate in your religious beliefs. I need you to respect that I don't share that faith, and that I don't want to be pressured to accept something I don't believe.

I want to be clear that I am not a religious person and will never convert to your faith. Please stop bringing it up and leaving materials out for me to read. I love you and want our relationship to work. Do you think it can work without me sharing your religious beliefs?

I'm open to discussing this more, if you have any questions. I want to know your thoughts.

Love,
Jason

Letter #76: I need you to participate in religious traditions more.

Dear Jason,

I love you, and I hope you'll take a few minutes to read this letter with an open mind. This is not an attempt to change your mind or coerce you into anything.

You have been clear about your beliefs and about not wanting to go to church with the kids and me. I respect your position, even though I wish it were different.

I'm writing to see if you would be willing to bend your stance slightly, and join us for a few special church traditions. Specifically, I'd like you to be with us for the Christmas Eve service, Easter Sunday, and when the kids participate in something special as part of their youth program. This would mean joining us at church five or six times a year.

I'm asking because these are family events that are meaningful to me and the children, and we want you there with us. It doesn't feel like a family without you. I'm not asking you to change your beliefs, just to support our family during these occasions.

Please think about my request and whether you can make this compromise without resentment. I promise, I am not trying to reel you in to becoming a regular church goer.

Let me know if you can do this, once you've had a chance to think it over.

Love,
Sarah

Section 20
Free Time

Letter #77: I feel resentful when you over-schedule our free time.

Dear Sarah,

I'm sorry I didn't act enthusiastic about the plans you made for the weekend. I do appreciate your efforts and the time you put into setting things up.

I need to be honest with you about my feelings related to our weekends and free time. You are a planner, and I know you like to have things lined up to do when we aren't working. I would rather not have our free time so scheduled.

I like having a stretch of time with nothing planned, so I can just relax and not rush to go anywhere or do anything. When you schedule our down time, it makes me feel overwhelmed and resentful. I don't want to hurt your feelings, because you put so much time into arranging plans, so I have been just going along when I would rather not.

From now on, I'm asking that you and I have a discussion before you begin making plans for us. I would like at least one day during the weekend when we do absolutely nothing, and I'd prefer not to go out more than one evening during the week.

I'm open to talking about this more. I just want you to understand my feelings, so we can work out something that feels good for both of us.

Love,
Jason

Letter #78: I need more time to myself.

Dear Jason,

I didn't mean to be rude last night when you came in and wanted to chat with me. I could tell I hurt you, and I'm so sorry. I was at the end of my book and wanted to finish it before bed.

This brings up something I want to share with you. I love you and love spending time with you. I want you to understand that as an introvert, I need more alone time than you might. As much as I love being with you, I also need time by myself. I need this time to think, process my day, and just recharge my batteries.

When we get home from work, I know you like to reconnect right away and talk about what happened during the day. Because I'm around people all day, when I get home I just want some time by myself, so I don't have to talk. I need about 30 minutes to unwind and relax by myself.

There are times when I want to go for a walk by myself or even go to a movie alone. This doesn't mean I don't love you or enjoy being with you. Having this alone time helps me take care of myself, so I can be a better wife to you.

I never want to hurt your feelings or seem like I'm pushing you away. That isn't my intention at all. I want to feel free to tell you what I need, and I want you to feel safe that I love being with you, even when I ask for time alone. Also, I want you to be able to say that you need time with me, if you feel disconnected.

How can I best tell you when I need to be alone so that it doesn't feel hurtful? Please write back and tell me what you think.

Love,
Sarah

Letter #79: I don't like taking vacations with your sister.

Dear Sarah,

I love your idea about taking a cruise for our vacation this year. I think that's a fantastic idea, and I really appreciate you doing all the research.

I need to be honest about one part of the trip that I'm not excited about. During the past few years, we've vacationed with your sister and her husband. I would prefer not to vacation with them again. You and Anna are so close, and I know you enjoy having that time with her. It just isn't fun for me.

I love your sister, and Bob and I get along well for short periods of time. I don't think we are a good match with them when it comes to spending several days together on vacation.

They tend to bicker with each other after the first couple of days, and that makes me uncomfortable. Also, you and Anna will go off by yourselves to do things, and that leaves me alone with Bob. He and I don't have much in common, so we both end up compromising what we really want to do. I want to spend my vacation time with you, not Bob.

I am happy for you and Anna to take a trip together by yourselves, and I don't mind having a short weekend getaway with the two of them. I don't want to take a weeklong vacation with them anymore.

Can you understand my feelings about this? Are you onboard with doing the cruise by ourselves? Please write back and let me know.

Love,
Jason

Letter #80: I feel you try to make me feel guilty for taking free time.

Dear Jason,

As you read this letter, please take a deep breath, and try to read it with a loving heart and an open mind. I need you to hear me on this.

I was really hurt today when I got home from shopping, and you were so snippy and sarcastic with me. I explained to you earlier in the week that I would be out with Tina until after lunch today. I'm not sure why you were so upset when I got home.

This is something that occurs more often than you might realize. When I take time for myself, you will get angry or make disparaging remarks to make me feel bad and selfish.

I understand it's tiring to spend time alone with the kids and how hard it is to get anything else done when you are watching them. That's true for both of us.

When you take free time to play tennis or meet up with friends, I try hard to be supportive and encouraging, because I know how important it is to have a break from work and kids.

I need that same support and encouragement from you. I always give you plenty of advance notice and make sure you don't have a conflict with my plans. We both need and deserve time to ourselves without feeling guilty or uncomfortable about it.

I'm asking you to please stop making hurtful or passive comments to me when I come home from being out. Can you be more encouraging and supportive of my need to have time for myself?

Please write back and let me know if you can honor my requests.

Love,
Sarah

Section 21
Addiction and Illness

Letter #81: I know you are an alcoholic, and you need treatment.

Dear Sarah,

I love you, and I because I do, I can't continue to pretend that your drinking is normal and okay.

After your behavior last night at the party, I won't stay silent any longer. You are an alcoholic. It's time for us to be honest about it and take action.

Your drinking is impacting our relationship. It is also affecting the kids when they see you behaving strangely, and when you're too hung over in the morning to tend to them.

They need their mom, and I need my wife back.

It's time for you to begin a twelve-step program, and we both need to be in counseling together. I will be right by your side to support you through this as you work to recover.

Are you willing to accept the truth about your drinking and take action to address it? Please let me know today.

Love,
Jason

Letter #82: I can no longer tolerate your drug abuse.

Dear Jason,

As much as I love you and want our marriage to work, I have reached the end of my rope with your drug addiction.

I am suffering too much and the anxiety of living with an addict is taking a huge toll on my mental and physical health.

I have made a call to a treatment center. You can be admitted this week as an in-patient for the 90-day program. You can go tomorrow.

If you are willing to go and stick with the treatment, I'm willing to stick with you through this. If you aren't willing, I can no longer stay married to you. I will need to know your answer today.

Love,
Sarah

Letter #83: I need help with my addiction.

Dear Sarah,

I love you so much—I want you to know that first and foremost.

I'm scared writing you this letter, because I don't know how you will react. This is a time I really need your help and support.

I have been lying to you about my pain meds. I haven't weaned myself off them like I told you a few months ago. Since my back surgery, I have continued to take them and have gotten more prescriptions from several different doctors.

I am so sorry I've lied to you. I feel so guilty about deceiving you and hope you will forgive me. The truth is, I can't stop taking them by myself. I've had to take more and more pills to control the pain, and when I've tried to stop, I have terrible withdrawal symptoms, which are excruciating. So, I keep taking them and finding doctors to write prescriptions.

I need help dealing with this, Sarah. I am so embarrassed that this has happened, and I hate that we have another big issue to face after going through the back problems and surgery.

I'm so depressed and scared, I don't know where to start or what to do. I always want to be strong for you, and I really need your help with this. Can you forgive me for lying and getting myself into this mess, and can you please support me through this?

Love,
Jason

Letter #84: Do you have a porn addiction?

Dear Jason,

I am really worried, and I don't know what's going on. I need you to be honest with me about something I've discovered.

I found a credit card statement in the bedroom that wasn't from one of our regular cards. It had your name on it. And when I looked it up, it was for a porn site. I looked at your computer history, and I'm freaking out. You are on this site every day.

What is going on with this? Are you addicted to porn? I have read a little about porn addiction, and I know it can be hard to control. Is this the situation with you?

Barrie Davenport

I am scared and hurt and wonder why you need to watch porn videos every day. I need you to be upfront with me, Jason, so we can figure this out.

Please write back quickly and be truthful with me. If there is a problem, we need to address it right away.

Love,
Sarah

Conclusion

"Communication to a relationship is like oxygen to life. Without it . . . it dies."

—Tony Gaskins

You and your partner need to communicate. You need to communicate in a way that reinforces your closeness and heals any wounds or misunderstandings. Communicating verbally can sometimes sabotage those relationship goals, especially when emotions run high.

Aggressiveness, blaming, defensiveness, criticism, shaming, sarcasm, stonewalling, and passive-aggressive words never invite resolution and mutual understanding. These kinds of words and reactions pull you further apart and corrode your intimacy and love.

You may lack the self-control in the heat of the moment to avoid these reactions during conversation—most of us do. But you can avoid them in writing, if you learn how to express yourself well.

The ability to write your feelings and needs in a measured and intentional way can set the tone for healthier dialogue and help you and your partner bypass hurtful words and angry reactions. Letter writing allows you to slow down, think about your words, and articulate them in the spirit of love and kindness, even with the most difficult and painful situations.

As you become more skilled at healthy and mature communication through letters, you will also find that dialogue becomes easier. You and your partner will learn a new way to respond verbally to each other that isn't as reactive or uncomfortable, by emulating your letter writing style.

You will find it eventually becomes easier to speak the words you have been writing, as you have trained yourself to be more careful and thoughtful with what you say. When tempers flare or things get too uncomfortable, you can always revisit writing it out, rather than fighting it out.

Ultimately, you want the ability to talk to each other about anything, even the painful things, without the conversation devolving into arguments and hurt feelings.

This kind of face-to-face communication requires practice and courage, but it has the most potential for growth and healing in your marriage or intimate relationship. I have included some resources in the next section related to verbal communication that will help you strengthen this area in your relationship.

I hope you have found these letter writing templates helpful and that you've identified phrases and ideas that are relevant to some of the challenges and issues in your relationship. If there are relationship issues or letter writing ideas that you would like to share with me, I would love hearing from you. Please email me at support@barriedavenport.com.

Also, please check out the Support Resources section in this book for more materials on healthy relationship communication.

Barrie Davenport

Support Resources

Write It Out, Don't Fight It Out **Companion Site**
liveboldandbloom.com/write-not-fight

Couples Communication Course
liveboldandbloom.com/communication-course

Live Bold and Bloom Relationship Articles
http://liveboldandbloom.com/category/relationships

201 Relationship Questions: The Couple's Guide to Building Trust and Emotional Intimacy
liveboldandbloom.com/201-questions

The Seven Principles for Making Marriage Work: A Practical Guide from the Country's Foremost Relationship Expert, John Gottman

Barrie Davenport

References

Why Letter Writing Works and When to Use It

Murray, Bridget. (2002). "Writing to Heal." *Monitor on Psychology 33,* no. 6.

Lisitsa, Ellie. (2012). "The Positive Perspective: Dr. Gottman's Magic Ratio!" The Gottman Institute.

Davenport, Barrie. "Six Love Letters That Create a Sexier, Happier Relationship." Live Bold and Bloom.

Why Conflict Is Valuable

University of Michigan. (2010). "Predicting Divorce: Study Shows How Fight Styles Affect Marriage." *ScienceDaily.*

Common Relationship Conflict Areas

Gottman, John M. (2000). *The Seven Principles for Making Marriage Work: A Practical Guide from the Country's Foremost Relationship Expert.* Harmony.

Pew Research Center. (2007). "As Marriage and Parenthood Drift Apart, Public Is Concerned about Social Impact."

Communication Killers That Make Talking Impossible

Barker, Eric. "The Four Most Common Relationship Problems—and How to Fix Them."

"Gottman Couples and Marital Therapy." Couples Training Institute.

Using Anger as a Warning

Spiegel, Alex. (2009). "Does Getting Angry Make You Angrier?" *NPR*.

Brown, Brené. (2010). *The Gifts of Imperfection: Let Go of Who You Think You're Supposed to Be and Embrace Who You Are.* Hazelden Publishing.

Did You Like
Write It Out,
Don't Fight It Out?

Thank you so much for purchasing *Write It Out, Don't Fight It Out: How to Use Letters to Heal Your Relationship When Talking Gets Tough.* I'm honored by the trust you've placed in me and my work by choosing this book to better understand relationship communication and how to improve it in your own relationship. I truly hope you've enjoyed it and found it useful for your life.

I'd like to ask you for a small favor. Would you please take just a minute to leave a review for this book on Amazon? This feedback will help me continue to write the kind of books that will best serve you. If you really loved the book, please let me know!

Barrie Davenport

Other Books You Might Enjoy from Barrie Davenport

201 Relationship Questions: The Couple's Guide to Building Trust and Emotional Intimacy
(liveboldandbloom.com/201-questions)

Emotional Abuse Breakthrough: How to Speak Up, Set Boundaries, and Break the Cycle of Manipulation and Control with Your Abusive Partner
(liveboldandbloom.com/eab-book)

Emotional Abuse Breakthrough Scripts: 107 Empowering Responses and Boundaries to Use with Your Abuser
(liveboldandbloom.com/ea-scripts)

Signs of Emotional Abuse: How to Recognize the Patterns of Narcissism, Manipulation, and Control in Your Love Relationship
(liveboldandbloom.com/signsea)

Building Confidence: Get Motivated, Overcome Social Fear, Be Assertive, and Empower Your Life for Success
(liveboldandbloom.com/building-confidence)

Peace of Mindfulness: Everyday Rituals to Conquer Anxiety and Claim Unlimited Inner Peace
(liveboldandbloom.com/mindfulness-post)

Finely Tuned: How to Thrive as a Highly Sensitive Person or Empath
(liveboldandbloom.com/finely-tuned)

Self-Discovery Questions: 155 Breakthrough Questions to Accelerate Massive Action
(liveboldandbloom.com/questions-book)

Confidence Hacks: 99 Small Actions to Massively Boost Your Confidence
(liveboldandbloom.com/confidence-hacks)

10-Minute Declutter: The Stress-Free Habit for Simplifying Your Home
(liveboldandbloom.com/10-min-declutter)

10-Minute Digital Declutter: The Simple Habit to Eliminate Technology Overload
(liveboldandbloom.com/digital-declutter)

10-Minute Mindfulness: 71 Habits for Living in the Present Moment
(liveboldandbloom.com/10mm-book)

Declutter Your Mind: How to Stop Worrying, Relieve Anxiety, and Eliminate Negative Thinking
(liveboldandbloom.com/declutter-mind)

Sticky Habits: How to Achieve Your Goals without Quitting and Create Unbreakable Habits Starting with Five Minutes a Day
(liveboldandbloom.com/habits-book)

The 52-Week Life Passion Project: Uncover Your Life Passion
(liveboldandbloom.com/life-passion-book)

Made in the USA
Lexington, KY
21 November 2017